Put Downs

A Collection of Acid Wit

Laura Ward

PRC

Produced in 2004 by
PRC Publishing Limited
The Chrysalis Building
Bramley Road, London W10 6SP

An imprint of **Chrysalis** Books Group

This edition published in 2004
Distributed in the U.S. and Canada by:
Sterling Publishing Co., Inc.
387 Park Avenue South
New York, NY 10016

ISBN 1 85648 722 9

Printed and bound in Malaysia

Contents

Introduction

Every normal man must be tempted at times to spit on his hands,

    hoist the black flag, and begin slitting throats.

        H. L. Mencken

There's invariably a moment in all of our lives when we reach the point where we've had enough of being nice, of saying the right thing, minding our Ps and Qs, and stop and think—hang it all, let's just say what we really mean. We've been elbowed and jostled, talked over, talked down to, and metaphorically pushed and shoved in so many directions and on more occasions than the spirit can stand. So, we muster our resolve—there is no more playing nicely with our fellow citizens; it's gloves-off and down in the mud.

It's thus in a spirit of awe coupled with no small amount of envy that this collection of perfect put downs has been assembled. As a dilution of the nastiest, cleverest, and most astonishingly vituperative comebacks and condemnations ever pronounced, there will be many familiar names—masters and mistresses of the perfect barb—between these covers, as well as some verbal broadsides from unexpected quarters (those otherwise placid souls pushed to breaking point).

A great put-down can come in a variety of guises and shades (of crimson, puce—surely, to my mind, it would take a livid color...). For example, it can take the form of a spilling-over of boiling rage, so majestic and overwhelming that it leaves even its victim reeling in admiration, or the casual sideswipe that leaves the target dazed, severely grazed, and confused. It can have the delayed detonation of a very long fuse wire, or the sudden impact of a megaton bomb.

The trouble for most of us (and certainly in so as far as my own experience goes) is that when it comes to it, so often the mouth just won't play ball. Either something incredibly dumb and ineffectual slips out, leaving "the target" laughing at such a feeble attempt at verbal abuse, or words seem to fail altogether and remain empty thought bubbles in the air. Whichever, the net result is the same. Flailing desperately about, at moments like these some inspiration from those whose verbal weaponry and mental acuity are sharpened to a fine point (a pointed put-down, in point of fact) is sorely needed.

Where the long fuse wire—where you could almost count to ten before the insult is unleashed–is concerned, there's the perfect example of Dorothy Parker. She knocked down the pompous individual who had declared "I can't bear fools," with the ingenue-like response, "That's queer. Your mother could." Or the writer Eugene Field whom, in a rejection note to the aspiring author of a poem entitled, "Why do I live?" answered matter-of-factly: "Because you send your poem by mail." For that one, you'd need to count to twenty...

As for the dynamite effect, there are numerous examples of bile unleashed with explosive results. Take the Romantic poet Lord Byron ("mad, bad, and dangerous to know") who could really work himself into a frenzied onslaught. In a letter to John Murray in 1818, he attacked fellow poet John Keats: "Here are Johnny Keats's piss-a-bed poetry... No more Keats, I entreat: flay him alive; if some of you don't I must skin him myself: there is no bearing the drivelling idiotism of the Mankin." Meanwhile, to an unkind critic, the Scottish poet Robert Burns railed: "Thou eunuch of language, thou pimp of gender, murderous accoucheur of infant learning, thou pickle-herring in the puppet show of nonsense." Poets certainly seem to have a particular flair for such splendid invective, piling up phrases until the volume reaches a spectacular fever pitch.

The style of delivery may vary, but the substance remains the same: a verbal attack or counter-attack delivered with flair, imagination, precision, and wit. For a perfect put down is not just being rude for the sake of being rude; after all, there are plenty of unpleasant and boorish people about. It's a quick riposte or flight of repartee delivered in such a way that it enriches our very language, and spices up the lives of those of us who are not so linguistically blessed.

It can also, in the case of a vitriolic personal attack, be something of a cathartic release (for the bystander, that is to say, not the person on the receiving end...). For one can only step aside and marvel, agog, and with a mounting sense of exhilaration, at the verbal ingenuity of someone like William Makepeace Thackeray as he lays into the English writer Jonathan Swift (author of *Gulliver's Travels*). He launches in, conjuring up quite an outlandish spectacle of "A monster gibbering shrieks, and gnashing imprecations against mankind—tearing down all shreds of modesty, past all sense of manliness and shame; filthy in word, filthy in thought, furious, raging, obscene." Well that's telling 'em, well and good.

One can only wonder how such a stream of venom was received; the volley is so exaggerated, conveys such a maelstrom of emotion, as almost to disappear inside its own deadly vortex, perhaps consuming its deliverer more than its intended target. Viz, the typically–and endlessly–vitriolic Victorian critic John Ruskin, on this occasion giving his two bits' worth on the German composer Wagner:

"Of all the bête, clumsy, blundering, boggling, baboon-blooded stuff that I ever saw on a human stage, that last night beat—as far as the story and acting went—all the affected, sapless, soulless, beginningless, endless, topless, bottomless, topsiturviest, tuneless, scrabble-pipiest-tongs, and boniest-doggerel of sounds I ever endured the deadliness of, that eternity of nothing was deadliest, as far as its sound went."

Richard Wagner spoke very highly of him too, no doubt... To my mind, though, the most pleasing of put downs is the casual (dare one say, almost good-natured?) slight. Or perhaps the latter just seems more in tune with our present penchant for capsule criticism, off-the-cuff cleverness, and the voguish sound bite, and someday no doubt we'll revert to bile of magisterial, Shakespearean proportions. (Though, if all the world is indeed a stage, Queen Margaret in Shakespeare's *Richard III*, railing against "that bottled spider, that poisonous bunchback'd toad" would surely have a pithy put down to hand about some key players on the contemporary scene.)

Snappy put downs and comebacks appeal partly, perhaps, for their drop of humanity, for being less electrically charged with the personal, and, rather, overflowing with casual, all-encompassing cynicism. Yet they are no less honed (or spiked!) and polished for all that—from whence some of the most memorable one-liners.

Thus alongside the verbal jousting, venting of spleen, and cantankerous curmudgeons, one finds the more detached, conversational wit so thoroughly embodied by Oscar Wilde (to whit, Oscar's remark, "He gets invited to all the Great Houses of England–once"). And the in-passing, devastating humor of a comment such as that made by Mark Twain of J. M. W. Turner's painting *The Slave Ship*: "It resembles a tortoiseshell cat having a fit in a platter of tomatoes." Or the writer and wit Noël Coward, who responded to an actor who had asked him anxiously after a performance, "Could you see my wig join?" with the "reassuring" comment: "Perfectly, my dear boy, perfectly." Turning up the venom dial on the theater wavelength, there's W. S. Gilbert (of Gilbert and Sullivan fame) on Herbert Beerbohm Tree's performance as Hamlet: "My dear fellow, I never saw anything so funny in my life, and yet it was not in the least bit vulgar." And George S. Kaufman's casual, "Ah, forgotten but not gone," to a Hollywood producer who had supposedly left town.

All of this is well and good–so long as you're not in the line of fire. As Alexander Woollcott wrote (in *While Rome Burns*) of Dorothy

Parker's poems, stories, and criticisms: "[They] have delighted everyone except those about whom they were written." Or, for a down-to-earth analogy, there is the English author P. G. Wodehouse, who said of shooting as a sport, "The fascination... depends almost wholly on whether you are at the right or wrong end of the gun."

So, while working hard to stay the right end of the gun and hopefully avoiding stray bullets, perhaps, like me, you'll take a word of advice from Groucho Marx's sober summary. Of the famous "Round Table" at the Algonquin Hotel in New York, so prominent in the literary life of that city in the twenties and thirties (and home from home for Parker, Woollcott, Kaufman, and Co.), Groucho put it this way: "The admission fee was a viper's tongue and a half-concealed stiletto. It was a sort of intellectual slaughterhouse." This, then, is territory where angels might fear to tread.

With this in mind, it's hoped this collection of put downs will prove entertaining and provide food for thought—and, for the intrepid (or foolhardy), possibly even sharpen the tongue and teeth to provide the perfect weaponry for future verbal jousts. For most of us, once we've let off steam, generally we go back to our habitual daily pattern, satisfied that a point has been made, and that it has—hopefully—hit home. So we return to the business of trying to climb the ladder of success, rung by rung (or wrong by wrong... to steal a famous quip from between these covers), of suffering fools and the like without too much complaint. With a sneaking respect for those who manage to raise such ripostes to an art form.

Laura Ward

March 2004

" Writers "

Dedicated to the Warden and Fellow of St Antony's College, Oxford—Except one.

Dedication by Jan Morris in her book on Oxford

She looked like Lady Chatterley above the waist and the gamekeeper below.

Cyril Connolly, on Vita Sackville-West, whose attire often consisted of twinset and pearls plus gaiters...

I do not think I have ever seen a nastier-looking man... Under the black hat, when I had first seen them, the eyes had been those of an unsuccessful rapist.

Ernest Hemingway, describing the British poet and artist Percy Wyndham Lewis

He festooned the dung heap on which he had placed himself with sonnets as people grow honeysuckle around outdoor privies.

Quentin Crisp, on Oscar Wilde

People who like this sort of thing will find this the sort of thing they like.

Abraham Lincoln, in a review of a book

A great zircon in the diadem of American literature.

Gore Vidal, on Truman Capote

Truman Capote has made lying an art. A minor art.

Gore Vidal

He's a full-fledged housewife from Kansas with all the prejudices.

Gore Vidal, on Truman Capote

Truman Capote's death was a good career move.

Gore Vidal

It was a book to kill time for those who liked it better dead.

Rose Macaulay

Even those who call Mr. Faulkner our greatest literary sadist do not fully
    appreciate him, for it is not merely his characters who have to run the
    gauntlet but also his readers.

Clifton Fadiman, on William Faulkner

He uses a lot of big words, and his sentences are from here to the airport.

Carolyn Chute, on William Faulkner

He was a great friend of mine. Well, as much as you could be a friend of his,
unless you were a fourteen-year-old nymphet.

Truman Capote, on William Faulkner

He has never been known to use a word that might send a reader to the
dictionary.

William Faulkner, on Ernest Hemingway

Poor Faulkner. Does he really think big emotions come from big words? He
thinks I don't know the ten-dollar words. I know them all right. But there are
older and simpler and better words, and those are the ones I use.

Ernest Hemingway, about William Faulkner

Anyone who doesn't like this book is healthy.

Groucho Marx, on Oscar Levant's The Memoirs of an Amnesiac

Many thanks. I shall lose no time in reading it.

Benjamin Disraeli, to an aspiring author who had sent him a manuscript

That hyena in petticoats.

Horace Walpole, of Mary Wollstonecraft, in a letter to Hannah More, 1795

An animated adenoid.

Norman Douglas, English novelist, on fellow English writer
Ford Madox Ford

Take from him his sophisms, futilities, and incomprehensibilities and what
remains? His foggy mind.

Thomas Jefferson, on Plato

Gibbon is an ugly, affected, disgusting fellow and poisons our literary club for
me. I class him among infidel wasps and venomous insects.

James Boswell, about Edward Gibbon, English historian

Always willing to lend a helping hand to the one above him.

F. Scott Fitzgerald, on Ernest Hemingway

The stupid person's idea of the clever person.

Elizabeth Bowen, British writer, on Aldous Huxley,
in the Spectator *magazine, 1936*

He had a mind so fine that no idea could violate it.

T. S. Eliot, about Henry James

I have just read a long novel by Henry James. Much of it made me think of the
priest condemned for a long space to confess nuns.

W. B. Yeats, Irish poet, on Henry James

A little emasculated mass of inanity.

Theodore Roosevelt, about Henry James

I am reading Henry James... and feel myself as one entombed in a block of
smooth amber.

Virginia Woolf, about Henry James

...a flabby lemon and pink giant, who hung his mouth open as though he were
an animal at the zoo inviting buns–especially when the ladies were present.

Percy Wyndham Lewis, British poet and artist,
on fellow Brit Ford Madox Ford

There is no arguing with Johnson; for when his pistol misses fire, he knocks you
down with the butt end of it.

Oliver Goldsmith, about Samuel Johnson

That's not writing, that's typing.

Truman Capote, about Jack Kerouac's style in On The Road

An unmanly sort of man whose love life seems to have been largely confined to
crying in laps and playing mouse.

W. H. Auden, British poet, on Edgar Allan Poe

Mr. Lawrence looked like a plaster gnome on a stone toadstool in some
suburban garden . . . he looked as if he had just returned from spending an
uncomfortable night in a very dark cave.

Dame Edith Sitwell, British poet, about D. H. Lawrence

A tall, thin, spectacled man with the face of a harassed rat.

Russell Maloney, about James Thurber

A monster gibbering shrieks, and gnashing imprecations against mankind—

tearing down all shreds of modesty, past all sense of manliness and shame;

filthy in word, filthy in thought, furious, raging, obscene.

William Makepeace Thackeray on 18th-century English writer

Jonathan Swift, author of Gulliver's Travels

Fine words! I wonder where you stole them.

Jonathan Swift

Thackeray settled like a meat-fly on whatever one had got for dinner, and made

one sick of it.

John Ruskin, Fors Clavigera, *Letter xxxi*

The Cynic Parasite.

Benjamin Disraeli, on William Makepeace Thackeray

His sayings are generally like women's letters; all the pith is in the postscript.

William Hazlitt, on Charles Lamb, British essayist and writer

The Hitler of the book racket.

Wyndham Lewis, British writer and artist, on Arnold Bennett,

British novelist

All that expert help...has still not managed to correct her apparent belief that Trafalgar came shortly before Waterloo; perhaps she has confused English history with the London Underground system.

> *Bernard Levin, on the novel* Love at the Helm *by the doyen of romantic literature, Barbara Cartland (Lord Mountbatten had, apparently, assisted with the book...)*

Oh, I see—one a year.

> *Denise Robins to fellow romantic novelist Barbara Cartland, who had told her that she had written 145 books*

It makes me feel masculine to tell you that I do not answer questions like this without being paid for answering them.

> *Lillian Hellman, asked by* Harper's *magazine in which situation she felt most masculine*

I can't understand why a person will take a year or two to write a novel when he can easily buy one for a few dollars.

> *Fred Allen*

Kipling is a jingo imperialist, he is morally insensitive and aesthetically disgusting.

> *George Orwell, on Rudyard Kipling*

Madame: I was told that you took the trouble to come here to see me three
times last evening. I was not in. And, fearing lest persistence expose you to
humiliation, I am bound by the rules of politeness to warn you that I shall
never be in.

> *Gustave Flaubert, in a letter to Louise Colet,*
> *his sometime mistress. (She riposted with the words,*
> *lâche – feeble – couard – coward – and canaille – scum.)*

A great cow of ink.

> *Gustave Flaubert, of fellow French writer George Sand (*nom de
> plume *of Amantine Aurore Dudevant)*

George Eliot had the heart of Sappho; but the face, with the long proboscis, the
protruding teeth of the Apocalyptic horse, betrayed animality.

> *George Meredith, English novelist and poet,*
> *on George Eliot (Mary Ann Evans)*

A hack writer who would not have been considered a fourth rate in Europe,
who tricked out a few of the old proven "sure-fire" literary skeletons with
sufficient local color to intrigue the superficial and the lazy.

> *William Faulkner, on Mark Twain*

Nothing but a pack of lies.

> *Damon Runyon on* Alice in Wonderland *by Lewis Carroll*

I was too polite to ask.

> *Gore Vidal, when asked whether his first sexual encounter had*
> *been male or female*

When his cock wouldn't stand up he blew his head off. He sold himself a line of
bulls**t, and bought it.

> *Germaine Greer, on Ernest Hemingway*

The trouble with Ian is that he gets off with women because he can't get on
with them.

> *Rosamond Lehmann, of fellow author Ian Fleming, creator of the*
> *fictional hero James Bond*

No one reads him, they hear of him.

> *Gore Vidal, of Norman Mailer*

Once again, words have failed Norman.

> *Gore Vidal, on Norman Mailer, who had thrown his drink over*
> *Vidal when the latter stubbornly refused to rise to the bait*
> *—their literary animosity became famous*

He has the most remarkable and seductive genius—and I should say about the
smallest in the world.

> *Lytton Strachey, on Max Beerbohm*

Pro-crypto Nazi.

> *Gore Vidal to William F. Buckley Jr., in a televised debate on*
> *August 22, 1968—with ABC newsman Howard K. Smith stuck in*
> *the middle. To the above comment, Buckley responded with:*
> *"Now listen, you queer, stop calling me a crypto-Nazi or I'll sock*
> *you in your goddamn face and you'll stay plastered."'*

A lady magazine writer...

> *Lillian Hellman, of Mary McCarthy*

[Hellman] is tremendously overrated, a bad writer, and a dishonest
   writer...[whose every written word] is a lie, including "and" and "the."

> *Mary McCarthy, of Lillian Hellman, in an interview*
> *with Dick Cavett on the* Dick Cavett Show *in 1980*

In historical and political matters you are partisan of a certain interpretation
   which you regard as absolute.

> *Vladimir Nabokov, on Edmund Wilson*

Gertrude Stein was never crazy
Gertrude Stein was very lazy.

> *Ernest Hemingway, quoted in* Literary Feuds, *by Anthony Arthur*

I still say you [Theodore Dreiser] are a liar and a thief.

> *Sinclair Lewis*

He [Sinclair Lewis] is noisy, ostentatious, and shallow... I never could like
the man.

Theodore Dreiser

I denounce Mr. Bernard De Voto as a fool and a tedious and egotistical fool, as a
liar and a pompous and boresome liar.

Sinclair Lewis

It is inhuman to attack [Truman] Capote. You are attacking an elf.

Gore Vidal

[Reading a long novel by Thomas Wolfe is like] making love to a 300-pound
woman. Once she gets on top, it's all over. Fall in love or be asphyxiated.

Norman Mailer

The greatest mind ever to stay in prep school.

Norman Mailer, of J. D. Salinger

Features so horrid, were it light,
Would put the devil himself to flight.

*Charles Churchill, famous poet of the day, attacking
Dr. Samuel Johnson, whose rather grotesque appearance
was known to all (he nicknamed the Doctor "Pomposo"
in his poem* The Ghost, *from which this verse comes)*

The misfortune of Goldsmith in conversation is this: he goes on without
knowing how he is to get off.

> *Dr. Samuel Johnson, on fellow writer (author of*
> The Vicar of Wakefield*) Oliver Goldsmith*

Why, Sir, Sherry is dull, naturally dull; but it must have taken him a great deal of
pains to become what we now see him. Such an excess of stupidity, Sir, is not
in Nature.

> *Dr. Samuel Johnson, on Thomas Sheridan, English critic and poet*

They teach the morals of a whore, and the manners of a dancing master.

> *Dr. Samuel Johnson, on the* Letters to His Son *written by the Earl
> of Chesterfield; the book was a publishing sensation in its day*

An unattractive man with an apple-green complexion.

> *Steven Runciman, British historian, on André Gide, French novelist*

Dribble: long and continuous.

> *One reviewer's opinion of Norman Mailer's work* The Prisoner of Sex *(1971),
> an analysis of the women's movement*

[Mailer] wallows in self-pity, pride, and a world-historical egomania, thereby
providing an accurate portrait of the mental state of most writers most of
the time.

> *Judith Shulevitz, on Norman Mailer's notorious* Advertisements for Myself

Lady Chatterley's Lover—Mr. Lawrence has a diseased mind. He is obsessed by
sex and we have no doubt that he will be ostracized by all except the most
degenerate coteries of the world.

> John Bull *magazine, 1928*

My dear fellow, I may be dead from the neck up, but rack my brains as I may I
can't see why a chap should need thirty pages to describe how he turns over
in bed before going to sleep.

> *Rejection note from a publisher to Marcel Proust, on receiving the*
> *manuscript for the author's work* Swann's Way *(one part of*
> *what would become* Remembrance of Things Past*)*

Oh, really. What exactly is she reading?

> *Dame Edith Evans, on being told that the writer*
> *Nancy Mitford—author of* Love in a Cold Climate
> *—had been lent a villa in order to "finish her book"*

She preserved to the age of 56 that contempt for ideas which is normal among
boys and girls of fifteen.

> *Odell Shepherd, on Louisa May Alcott*

A fungus of pendulous shape.

> *Alice James, on George Eliot (pseudonym of Mary Ann Evans)*

To those she did not like... she was a stiletto made of sugar.

> *John Mason Brown, on Dorothy Parker*

28

In her last days, she resembled a spoiled pear.

Gore Vidal, on Gertrude Stein

Miss Stein was a past master in making nothing happen very slowly.

Clifton Fadiman, on Gertrude Stein

An immense priestess of nonsense expounding her text in nonsense syllables.

Alfred Kazin, on Gertrude Stein

The Young Men's Christian Association—with Christ left out, of course.

Gertrude Stein, on the Bloomsbury Group

All raw, uncooked, protesting.

Virginia Woolf, on Aldous Huxley

Virginia Woolf, I enjoyed talking to her, but thought nothing of her writing. I
considered her "a beautiful little knitter."

Dame Edith Sitwell, British poet

The author of this book is beyond psychiatric help.

An editor to J.G. Ballard, regarding the manuscript
for his novel Crash *(1973)*

Good God, I can't publish this. We'd both be in jail.

An editor to William Faulkner, regarding the
manuscript for his novel Sanctuary *(1931)*

My God, what a clumsy *olla putrida* James Joyce is! Nothing but old fags and
  cabbage-stumps of quotations from the Bible and the rest, stewed in the juice
  of deliberate, journalistic dirty-mindedness.

> *D. H. Lawrence, on James Joyce, author of* Ulysses, *in a letter to*
> *Aldous and Maria Huxley, August 15, 1928*

Your manuscript is both good and original; but the part that is good is not
  original, and the part that is original is not good.

> *Samuel Johnson*

Freud Madox Fraud.

> *Osbert Sitwell, on Ford Madox Ford*

So will Bernard Shaw.

> *George Bernard Shaw's response to an invitation that read*
> *along the lines of, "So-and-So will be at home on this date"*
> *—the lady having snubbed G. B. S. on an earlier occasion*

He is every other inch a gentleman.

> *Rebecca West, on novelist Michael Arlen; the quote*
> *is also attributed to Alexander Woollcott*

One of the nicest old ladies I ever met.

> *William Faulkner, on Henry James*

Lord Berners has left Lesbos for the Isle of Man.

> *Notice placed in the newspapers by said Lord Berners,*
> *about whom rumors were circulating that he might marry*
> *Violet Trefusis–"companion" of Vita Sackville-West*

His style has the desperate jauntiness of an orchestra fiddling away for dear life
on a sinking ship.

> *Edmund Wilson, on Evelyn Waugh, author of* Brideshead Revisited

He not only overflowed with learning, but stood in the slop.

> *Sydney Smith, on Thomas Babington Macaulay*

The work of a queasy undergraduate scratching his pimples.

> *Virginia Woolf, on James Joyce's* Ulysses

One cannot say she was dressed. She was clothed. And so uncertainly that it
was unsure she would remain even that.

> *Ivy Compton-Burnett, on a scantily clad female*

It is a reminder that [the yacht] *Morning Cloud's* skipper is no stranger to
platitude and longitude.

> *Christopher Wordswoth, from the* Observer *newspaper, on*
> *Edward Heath's sailing-based book* Travels

From the moment I picked your book up until I laid it down I was convulsed
with laughter. Someday I intend reading it.

> *Groucho Marx, about S. J. Perelman's* Dawn Ginsberg's Revenge

He had the compassion of an icicle and the generosity of a pawnbroker.

> *S. J. Perelman, on Groucho Marx*

No, it did a lot of other things, too.

> *The author James Joyce, turning down a fan who had*
> *asked to kiss the hand that wrote* Ulysses

The way Bernard Shaw believes in himself is very refreshing in these atheistic
days when so many people believe in no god at all.

> *Israel Zangwill, English author*

I'm sure the poor woman meant well but I wish she'd stick to recreating the
glory that was Greece and not muck about with dear old modern homos.

> *Noël Coward, on Mary Renault, who wrote*
> *historical fiction set in ancient Greece*

Alexander Woollcott (on signing a first edition of his latest book): "Ah, what is so
rare as a Woollcott first edition?"
Franklin P. Adams: "A Woollcott second edition."

> *Exchange between the US journalist Adams and writer Woollcott*

Because you send your poem by mail.

> *Eugene Field, in a rejection slip to an author who had sent him a*
> *poem for publication entitled* Why do I live?

I found nothing really wrong with this autobiography except poor choice of
subject.

> *Clifton Fadiman, critic, on Gertrude Stein's* Everybody's Autobiography

Valley of the Dolls–for the reader who has put away comic books but isn't ready
for editorials in the *Daily News*

> *Gloria Steinem, on Jacqueline Susann's book in the* New York Times

He is able to turn an unplotted, unworkable manuscript into an unplotted and
unworkable manuscript with a lot of sex.

> *Tom Volpe, critic, on Harold Robbins*

This is not at all bad, except as prose.

> *Gore Vidal, on* The Winds of War *by Herman Wouk*

For my part, I can rarely tell whether his characters are making love or playing
tennis.

> *Joseph Kraft, critic, on novelist William Faulkner*

I've had to smell your works from time to time, and that has helped me to
become an expert on intellectual pollution.

> *Norman Mailer, on Gore Vidal*

A literary style... of wearing false hair on the chest.

> *Max Eastman, author, on the prose style of Ernest Hemingway*

He's got hold of the red meat of the English language and turned it into hamburgers.

> *Richard Gordon, on Ernest Hemingway*

The covers of this book are too far apart.

> *Ambrose Bierce, renowned cynic and author of the* Devil's Dictionary

The ineffable dunce has nothing to say and says it with a liberal embellishment of bad delivery, embroidering it with reasonless vulgarities of attitude, gesture, and attire. There never was an impostor so hateful, a blockhead so stupid, a crank so variously and offensively daft. He makes me tired.

> *Ambrose Bierce, on Oscar Wilde*

The Pelican Brief is the turkey long.

> New York *magazine review of the John Grisham book*

Gertrude Stein's prose is a cold, black suet-pudding. We can represent it as a cold suet-roll of fabulously reptilian length. Cut it at any point, it is... the same heavy, sticky, opaque mass all through, and all along.

> *Percy Wyndham Lewis, British poet and painter,*
> *on the American author Gertrude Stein*

An idiot child screaming in a hospital.

H.G. Wells, English writer, on George Bernard Shaw

Lively diarrhoea.

Noël Coward, on writer Gertrude Stein

The elephantine capers of an obese mountebank.

William Inge, English playwright, on the writings
of G. K. Chesterton

The same old sausage, fizzing and sputtering in its own grease.

Henry James Sr., English theologian, on Thomas Carlyle,
Scottish historian and essayist

The more I read him, the less I wonder that they poisoned him.

Thomas Babington Macaulay, British historian, on the
Greek philosopher Socrates

A fat little flabby person, with the face of a baker, the clothes of a cobbler, the
size of a barrel maker, the manners of a stocking salesman, and the dress of
an innkeeper.

Victor de Balabin, on the French novelist Honoré de Balzac

Monsieur Zola is determined to show that if he has not genius, he can at least
be dull.

Oscar Wilde, on Émile Zola

He has not an enemy in the world, and none of his friends like him.

Oscar Wilde, on George Bernard Shaw

Too much gasbag.

D. H. Lawrence, on George Bernard Shaw

His brain is a half-inch layer of champagne poured over a bucket of Methodist
near-beer.

Benjamin de Cassères, on George Bernard Shaw

He would not blow his nose without moralising on conditions in the
handkerchief industry.

Cyril Connolly, British critic, on George Orwell

Chesteron is like vile scum on a pond... All his slop!

Ezra Pound, on G.K. Chesterton

Mr. Fitzgerald—I believe that is how he spells his name—seems to believe that
plagiarism begins at home.

*Zelda Fitzgerald, on her husband F. Scott Fitzgerald, in her
review of* The Beautiful and the Damned. *Recorded in
Nancy Milford's 1970 biography of Zelda*

Nature did her best to make Mrs.— a very charming woman, only poor Nature
was sadly thwarted.

Geraldine Jewsbury, writer, in a letter to Jane Welsh Carlyle

Politics

Too bad all the people who know how to run the country are busy driving cabs and cutting hair.

George Burns

He has a bungalow mind.

Woodrow Wilson, 28th US president, on Warren G. Harding,
his successor as president

He writes the worst English that I have ever encountered. It reminds me of a string of wet sponges; it reminds me of tattered washing on the line; it reminds me of stale bean soup, of college yells, of dogs barking idiotically through endless nights. It is so bad that a sort of grandeur creeps into it. It drags itself out of the dark abyss of pish and crawls insanely up the topmost pinnacle of posh. It is rumble and bumble. It is flap and doodle. It is balder and dash.

H. L. Mencken, on the prose style of Warren G. Harding, US president

Young bore to John Wilkes: "I was born between 12 and 1 on the first of January … isn't that strange?"

Wilkes's reply: "Not at all, you could only have been conceived on the first of April."

We have a president for whom English is a second language. He's like, "We have to get rid of dictators," but he's pretty much one himself... In America, we have orange alert, but what the hell does that mean? We're supposed to be afraid of Krishna? Of orange sorbet? Then it's like, "You can't go out and shop, it's too dangerous out there," but if that happens then the economy falls... The message is so mixed: "Be afraid, but not too afraid."

Robin Williams, blasting George W. Bush

We're here tonight because of the Shrub, you know who I'm talking about. George W. Bush, Jr. The W stands for "Where the Hell is it?" You know, you look at George W. and you realize that some men are born great, some achieve greatness, and some get it as a graduation gift.

Robin Williams

I just want to tell Hillary, or the artist formerly known as the First Lady, I just want you to know Dan Quayle is running for the New York Senate. The problem is he moved to New Jersey. I don't know. He was hoping for the commuter vote... Every so often you look at those guys and go, "Darwin was wrong."

Robin Williams, on Hillary Clinton

He has all the characteristics of a dog except loyalty.

Sam Houston, on Thomas Jefferson Green

I think, father, that many men who are called great patriots in the House of
Commons are really great humbugs. For my own part, when I get into
Parliament, I will pledge myself to no party, but write upon my forehead in
legible characters, "To Be Let."

Tom Sheridan, British politician, in a letter to Richard Brinsley
Sheridan. Sheridan Sr.'s reply: Under it, Tom, write "Unfurnished"

Pétain in petticoats.

Denis Healey, on Margaret Thatcher, British prime minister

Being attacked by [Sir] Geoffrey Howe is like being savaged by a dead sheep.

Denis Healey, speaking in the House of Commons in 1978

Like being flogged with a warm lettuce.

Paul Keating, the then Australian premier, on being
attacked by the leader of the opposition

The Prime Minister tells us she has given the French president a piece of her
mind, not a gift I would receive with alacrity.

Denis Healey, on Margaret Thatcher

Attila the Hen.

Clement Freud, on Margaret Thatcher

Mrs Thatcher is doing for monetarism what the Boston Strangler did for door-to-door salesmen.

Denis Healey

I cannot bring myself to vote for a woman who has been voice-trained to speak to me as though my dog has just died.

Keith Waterhouse, on Margaret Thatcher in 1979,
the eve of her first election victory

Peter Mandelson has the insolent manner of one born to the top rung but three.

Gore Vidal, on a British politician

I suppose that the Honorable Gentleman's hair, like his intellect, will recede into the darkness.

Paul Keating, the then Australian prime minister,
on member of the opposition Andrew Peacock

You look like an Easter Island statue with an arse full of razor blades.

Paul Keating, to Malcolm Fraser

The trouble with Senator Long is that he is suffering from halitosis of the intellect. That's presuming Emperor Long has an intellect.

Harold L. Ickes, on Huey Long

Dewey has thrown his diaper into the ring.

> *Harold L. Ickes, of the youthful presidential candidate*

My gardener may call me Alice, all New York taxi drivers may call me Alice, the policeman and the trashman may call me Alice, but you may call me Mrs. Longworth.

> *Alice Roosevelt Longworth, to Senator Joseph McCarthy,*
> *who had called her by her first name*

Reminds me of nothing so much as a dead fish before it has had time to stiffen.

> *George Orwell, on English politician Clement Atlee*

Never trust a man who combs his hair straight from his left armpit.

> *Alice Roosevelt Longworth, on Douglas MacArthur*

What makes him think a middle-aged actor, who's played with a chimp, could have a future in politics?

> *Ronald Reagan, about Clint Eastwood running for mayor of Carmel*

He is racist, he's homophobic, he's xenophobic, and he's a sexist. He's the perfect Republican candidate.

> *Bill Press, about Pat Buchanan*

If I were the Archangel Gabriel, I'm afraid you wouldn't be in my constituency.

> *Robert Menzies, Australian Premier, to a heckler who had said*
> *she wouldn't vote for him even if he were the Archangel Gabriel*

Voter: "You little pipsqueak, I could swallow you in one bite."

Douglas's reply: "And if you did, my friend, you'd have more brains in your belly than you have in your head."

Tommy Douglas, former premier of Saskatchewan

A sophistical [sic] rhetorician, enebriated with the exuberance of his own verbocity, and gifted with an egotistical imagination, that can at all times command an interminable and inconsistent series of arguments, to malign an opponent and to glorify himself.

Benjamin Disraeli, British prime minister, speaking of
William Gladstone in the House of Commons

If Gladstone fell into the Thames, that would be a misfortune, and if anybody pulled him out that, I suppose, would be a calamity.

Benjamin Disraeli, British prime minister, on his rival William Gladstone

Posterity will do justice to that unprincipled maniac...with his extraordinary mixture of envy, vindictiveness, hypocrisy, and superstition; and with his one commanding characteristic—whether Prime Minister or Leader of Opposition, whether preaching, praying, speechifying, or scribbling—never a gentleman!

Benjamin Disraeli, British prime minister, on William Gladstone

He has not a single redeeming defect.

Benjamin Disraeli, on William Gladstone

His temper naturally morose, has become licentiously peevish. Crossed in his cabinet, he insults the House of Lords, and plagues the most eminent of his colleagues with the crabbed malice of a maundering witch.

Benjamin Disraeli, on the Earl of Aberdeen

The Right Honorable Gentleman's smile is like the silver fittings on a coffin.

Benjamin Disraeli, on Sir Robert Peel, founder of the British police

The Right Honorable Gentleman is reminiscent of a poker. The only difference is that a poker gives off occasional signs of warmth.

Benjamin Disraeli, on Robert Peel

Today's public figures can no longer write their own speeches or books, and there is some evidence that they can't read them either.

Gore Vidal, on the current political climate in the United States

A crafty and lecherous old hypocrite whose very statue seems to gloat on the wenches as they walk the States House yard.

William Cobbett, on Benjamin Franklin

Any political party that can't cough up anything better than a treacherous brain-damaged old vulture like Hubert Humphrey deserves every beating it gets. They don't hardly make 'em like Hubert any more—but just to be on the safe side, he should be castrated anyway.

Hunter S. Thompson, about Hubert Humphrey

He sits there in senile dementia with a gangrene heart and rotting brain,
grimacing at every reform, chattering impotently at all things that are decent,
frothing, fuming, violently gibbering, going down to his grave in snarling
infamy... disgraceful, depraved... and putrescent.

Hiram Johnson, on Harrison Grey Otis

Simply a radio personality who outlived his prime.

Evelyn Waugh (attrib.), English novelist, on Winston Churchill

Winston Churchill: "I venture to say that my Right Honorable friend, so redolent
of other knowledge, knows nothing of farming. I'll even make a bet that she
doesn't know how many toes a pig has."

Lady Astor: "Oh, yes I do. Take off your little shoesies and have a look."

Earl of Sandwich, to John Wilkes: "I am convinced, Mr. Wilkes, that you will die
either of the pox or on the gallows."

John Wilkes, in reply: "That depends, Sir, on whether I embrace your mistress or
your principles."

*The famous exchange has been relayed in variant forms
but the sentiment remains the same.*

History buffs probably noted the reunion at a Washington party a few weeks
ago of three ex-presidents: Carter, Ford, and Nixon—See No Evil, Hear No Evil,
and Evil.

Robert J. Dole, in a speech

A pin-stripin' polo-playin' umbrella-totin' Ivy-leaguer, born with a silver spoon so
far in his mouth that you couldn't get it out with a crowbar.

Bill Baxley, about George W. Bush

He can't help it—he was born with a silver foot in his mouth.

Ann Richards, about George W. Bush

He's a Boy Scout with a hormone imbalance.

Kevin Phillips, about George W. Bush

If ignorance ever goes to $40 a barrel, I want drilling rights on George
Bush's head.

Jim Hightower

He is your typical smiling, brilliant, back-stabbing, bullshitting southern
nut-cutter.

Lane Kirkland, about Jimmy Carter

He is a man suffering from petrified adolescence.

Aneurin (Nye) Bevan, about Winston Churchill

He would kill his own mother just so that he could use her skin to make a drum
to beat his own praises.

*Margot Asquith (attrib.), second wife of British Prime Minister
Herbert Asquith, on Winston Churchill*

They are not fit to manage a whelk stall.

> *Winston Churchill, on the Labour Party in Britain in 1945,*
> *the year he was ousted by it*

I thought he was a young man of promise; but it appears he is a young man of promises.

> *Arthur Balfour, on Winston Churchill*

Winston has devoted the best years of his life to preparing his impromptu speeches.

> *Lord Birkenhead (F. E. Smith), on Winston Churchill*

Bill Clinton's foreign policy experience is pretty much confined to having had breakfast once at the International House of Pancakes.

> *Pat Buchanan*

I'm just sick and tired of presidents who jog. Remember, if Bill Clinton wins, we're going to have another four years of his white thighs flapping in the wind.

> *Arianna Huffington*

When I was president, I said I was a Ford, not a Lincoln. Well what we have now is a convertible Dodge.

> *Gerald Ford, about Bill Clinton*

President Clinton apparently gets so much action that every couple of weeks
they have to spray WD-40 on his zipper.

David Letterman

Clinton is a man who thinks international affairs means dating a girl from out of
town.

Tom Clancy, novelist

When he does smile, he looks as if he's just evicted a widow.

Mike Royko, about Bob Dole

Hark, when Gerald Ford was king
We were bored with everything.
Unemployment 6 percent,
What a boring president.
Nothing major needed fixin'
So he pardoned Richard Nixon.

Bill Strauss and Eliana Newport

He is so dumb he can't fart and chew gum at the same time.

Lyndon B. Johnson, on Gerald Ford

Jerry Ford is a nice guy, but he played too much football with his helmet off.

Lyndon B. Johnson, on Gerald Ford

He looks like the guy in a science fiction movie who is the first to see the
Creature.

David Frye, on Gerald R. Ford

I have never seen...so slippery, so disgusting a candidate.

Nat Hentoff, on Bill Clinton

He has never met a tax he hasn't hiked.

Jack Kemp, on Bob Dole

He turned out to be so many different characters he could have populated all of
War and Peace and still had a few people left over.

Herbert Mitgang, on Lyndon B. Johnson

Avoid all needle drugs—the only dope worth shooting is Richard Nixon.

Abbie Hoffman

He bleeds people. He draws every drop of blood and then drops them from a
cliff. He'll blame any person he can put his foot on.

Martha Mitchell, on Richard Nixon

He inherited some good instincts from his Quaker forebears, but by diligent
hard work, he overcame them.

James Reston, on Richard Nixon

He is a shifty-eyed goddamn liar... He's one of the few in the history of this country to run for high office talking out of both sides of his mouth at the same time and lying out of both sides.

Harry S. Truman, on Richard Nixon

He was like a kamikaze pilot who keeps apologizing for the attack.

Mary McGrory, on Richard Nixon

Here is a guy who's had a stake driven through his heart. I mean, really nailed to the bottom of the coffin with a wooden stake, and a silver bullet through the forehead for good measure—and yet he keeps coming back.

Ted Koppel, on Richard Nixon

I may not know much, but I know chicken s**t from chicken salad.

Lyndon B. Johnson, on a speech by Richard Nixon

I worship the quicksand he walks in.

Art Buchwald, on Richard Nixon

Nixon's motto was, if two wrongs don't make a right, try three.

Norman Cousins, on Richard Nixon

Sir Richard-the-Chicken-Hearted.

Hubert H. Humphrey, on Richard Nixon

Dan Quayle is more stupid than Ronald Reagan put together.

Matt Groening

If life were fair, Dan Quayle would be making a living asking "Do you want fries
   with that?"

John Cleese, British comic actor

A triumph of the embalmer's art.

Gore Vidal, about Ronald Reagan

Compared to the Clintons, Reagan is living proof that a Republican with half a
   brain is better than a Democrat with two.

P. J. O'Rourke

He doesn't die his hair—he's just prematurely orange.

Gerald Ford, about Ronald Reagan

Looks and sounds not unlike Hitler—but without the charm.

Gore Vidal, on William F. Buckley Jr.

He has a chance to make somebody move over on Mount Rushmore. He's
   working for his place on the coins and the postage stamps.

Henry Graff, on Ronald Reagan

I believe that Ronald Reagan will someday make this country what it once
was... an arctic wilderness.

Steve Martin

I think Nancy does most of his talking; you'll notice that she never drinks water
when Ronnie speaks.

Robin Williams, on Ronald Reagan

In the heat of a political lifetime, he innocently squirrels away tidbits of
misinformation and then, sometimes years later, casually drops them into his
public discourse, like gumballs in a quiche.

Lucy Howard, on Ronald Reagan

He is the cutlery man of Australian politics. He was born with a silver spoon in
his mouth, speaks with a forked tongue, and knifes his colleagues in the back.

*Bob Hawke, on Malcolm Fraser in 1975 (whom he
later succeeded as Australian premier)*

People say satire is dead. It's not dead; it's alive and living in the White House.
He makes a Macy's Thanksgiving Day float look ridiculous. I think he's slowly
but surely regressing into movies again. In his mind he's looking at dailies,
playing dailies over and over.

Robin Williams, on Ronald Reagan

The youthful sparkle in his eyes is caused by his contact lenses, which he keeps
   highly polished.

Sheila Graham, on Ronald Reagan

Washington could not tell a lie; Nixon could not tell the truth; Reagan cannot tell
   the difference.

Mort Sahl

He's proof that there's life after death.

Mort Sahl, on Ronald Reagan

It has been the political career of this man to begin with hypocrisy, proceed
   with arrogance, and finish with contempt.

Thomas Paine, on John Adams

A nonentity with side whiskers.

Woodrow Wilson, on Chester A. Arthur

One could not even dignify him with the name of stuffed shirt. He was simply a
   hole on the air.

George Orwell, on Stanley Baldwin

He occasionally stumbled over the truth, but hastily picked himself up and
   hurried on as if nothing had happened.

Winston Churchill, on Stanley Baldwin

He has the lucidity which is the by-product of a fundamentally sterile mind.

Aneurin Bevan, on Neville Chamberlain

He looks as though he's been weaned on a pickle.

Alice Roosevelt Longworth, on Calvin Coolidge

Calvin Coolidge didn't say much, and when he did he didn't say much.

Will Rogers, on Calvin Coolidge

Young girl to Calvin Coolidge, the US president famous for his taciturnity: "Oh,
Mr President, Poppa says if I can get three words out of you he will buy me a
fur coat."

Coolidge's reply: "You lose."

He's the only man able to walk under a bed without hitting his head.

Walter Winchell, columnist, on Thomas E. Dewey

You really have to get to know him to dislike him.

James T. Patterson, on Thomas E. Dewey

He is just about the nastiest little man I've ever known. He struts sitting down.

Mrs Clarence Dykstra, on Thomas E. Dewey

Why, this fellow don't know any more about politics than a pig knows about
Sunday.

Harry S. Truman, on Dwight D. Eisenhower

He could not see a belt without hitting below it.

Margot Asquith, on David Lloyd George

It's great to be with Bill Buckley because you don't have to think. He takes a
position and you automatically take the opposite and you know you are right.

J. K. Galbraith

Hubert Humphrey talks so fast that listening to him is like trying to read
Playboy magazine with your wife turning the pages.

Barry Goldwater

His speeches left the impression of an army of pompous phrases moving over
the landscape in search of an idea.

William McAdoo, on Warren Harding

She is a four-million-dollar * * * * *—I can't say it, but it rhymes with rich.

Barbara Bush, on Geraldine Ferraro

He wouldn't commit himself to the time of day from a hatful of watches.

Westbrook Pegler, on Herbert Hoover

Such a little man could not have made so big a depression.

Norman Thomas, on Herbert Hoover

The hustler from Chicago.

George Bush, on Jesse Jackson

We make fun of George W. Bush, but this morning he was at work bright and
   early. Okay, he was early.

Jay Leno

We know that he has, more than any other man, the gift of compressing the
   largest amount of words into the smallest amount of thought.

Winston Churchill, on Ramsay MacDonald

He has no more backbone than a chocolate eclair.

Louise Lamprey, about President McKinley

The right honorable and learned gentleman has twice crossed the floor of this
   House, each time leaving behind a trail of slime.

David Lloyd George, British prime minister, on Sir John Simon

He has sat so long upon the fence that the iron has entered into his soul.

David Lloyd George, British prime minister, on Sir John Simon

When they circumcised Herbert Samuel, they threw away the wrong bit.

David Lloyd George, British prime minister, on a fellow politician

He was a good Lord Mayor of Birmingham in an off year.

David Lloyd George, on Neville Chamberlain

Dangerous as an enemy, untrustworthy as a friend, but fatal as a colleague.

Sir Hercules Robinson, on Joseph Chamberlain

He spoke for a hundred and seventeen minutes—in which period he was
detected only once in the use of an argument.

Arnold Bennett, on David Lloyd George

To hell with you. Offensive letter follows.

Telegram sent to Sir Alec Douglas-Home

Canada has at last produced a political leader worthy of assassination.

Irving Layton, about Pierre Trudeau

To err is Truman.

A catchphrase that was doing the rounds in 1946

A senescent bimbo with a lust for home furnishings.

Barbara Ehrenreich, on Nancy Reagan

She has the eyes of Caligula and the mouth of Marilyn Monroe.

François Mitterand, President of France, on Margaret Thatcher

She's democratic enough to talk down to anyone.

Austin Mitchell, Labour MP, on Margaret Thatcher

A Byzantine logothete.

Theodore Roosevelt, on Woodrow Wilson

A taste for charming and cultivated friends and a tendency to bathe frequently causes in them the deepest suspicion.

Theodore Roosevelt, on members of the "Free Silver" movement

His idea of getting hold of the right end of the stick is to snatch it from the hands of somebody who is using it effectively, and to hit him over the head with it.

George Bernard Shaw, on Theodore Roosevelt

Nero fiddles, but Coolidge only snored.

H. L. Mencken, on Calvin Coolidge

Democracy is that system of government under which the people, having 35,717,342 native-born adult whites to choose from, including thousands who are handsome and many of whom are wise, pick out Coolidge to be head of state.

H. L. Mencken, on Calvin Coolidge

Hoover, if elected, will do one thing that is almost incomprehensible to the human mind: he will make a great man out of Coolidge.

Clarence Darrow, during the American presidential campaign of 1928

When I was a boy, I was told anybody could become President of the United States; I'm beginning to believe it.

Clarence Darrow

The enviably attractive nephew who sings an Irish ballad for the company and
then winsomely disappears before the table clearing and dishwashing begin.

Lyndon B. Johnson, on John F. Kennedy

No, Mr. Chancellor, I was born in a manger.

President Lyndon B. Johnson to Ludwig Erhard of West Germany,
who had said, "I understand you were born in a log cabin."

I know he is, and he adores his creator.

Benjamin Disraeli, on being told that John Bright, a Quaker
radical from Rochdale, England, was a self-made man
(also attributed as being by Bright, of Disraeli)

Nixon is the kind of politician who would cut down a redwood tree and then
mount the stump to make a speech for conservation.

Adlai Stevenson, on Richard Nixon (attrib.)

Trust him as much as you would trust a rattlesnake with a silencer on its rattle.

Dean Acheson, on J. Edgar Hoover

Richard Nixon is a no-good lying b*****d. He can lie out of both sides of his
mouth at the same time and if he ever caught himself telling the truth he'd lie
just to keep his hand in.

Harry S. Truman

The General is suffering from mental saddle sores.

Harold L. Ickes, US Secretary of the Interior,
on Hugh S. Johnson, American soldier

He never commanded more than ten men in his life—and he ate three of them.

General Weston, on Adolphus W. Greely being made a general (Greely had
previously been an Arctic explorer...)

He is going around the country stirring up apathy.

William Whitelaw, British Conservative politician, on Harold Wilson
during the 1970 general election campaign

Greater love hath no man than this, that he lay down his friends for his life.

Jeremy Thorpe, Liberal member of parliament, passing comment
on Prime Minister Harold Macmillan's having fired half his
cabinet in the "Night of the Long Knives" in 1962

In the Bob Hope Golf Classic, the participation of President Gerald Ford was more than enough to remind you that the nuclear button was at one stage at the disposal of a man who might have either pressed it by mistake or else pressed it deliberately in order to obtain room service.

Clive James, Australian-born critic

He's done more U-turns than a dodgy plumber.

Iain Duncan Smith, Conservative leader, on the attitude of the
Prime Minister Tony Blair toward Europe

I'm not going to rearrange the furniture on the deck of the *Titanic*.

> *Rogers Morton, aide to President Ford, in response to those*
> *asking whether he was going to make any final adjustments*
> *in order to salvage the Ford re-election campaign of 1976*

A head like a banana and hips like a woman.

> *Hugh Dalton, British politician, on the French president Charles de Gaulle*

I think the last book that Nancy read was *Black Beauty*.

> *Roger Strauss, Democrat, on the intellectual quotient of Nancy Reagan*

They don't have a page that broad.

> *Gennifer Flowers, alleged mistress of Bill Clinton and* Penthouse *pinup,*
> *on why Hillary Clinton couldn't "bare her butt in any magazine"*

That slick, draft-dodging, dope-smoking, no-inhaling, philandering, Elvis-worshipping, Moscow-visiting, special-interest catering, Big-Mac-loving, hen-pecked, fork-tongued, Ivy League lawyer.

> *Michael Dalton Johnson, founder of* Slick Times, *on Bill Clinton*

I always said Little Truman had a voice so high it could only be detected by a bat.

> *Tennessee Williams, playwright, on Harry Truman*

They couldn't pour p**s out of a shoe if the instructions were written on the heel.

Lyndon B. Johnson, on the Association of American States

When they call the role in the Senate, the senators do not know whether to answer "present" or "not guilty."

Theodore Roosevelt

An empty suit that goes to funerals and plays golf.

Ross Perot, independent presidential candidate, on Dan Quayle

Dan Quayle is so dumb he thinks Cheerios are doughnut seeds.

Jim Hightower, Texan commentator

I wonder who wrote all those long words for him.

Mario Cuomo, New York governor, after Dan Quayle labeled him "liberalism's sensitive philosopher king"

[Dan Quayle] thinks that Roe v. Wade are two ways to cross the Potomac.

Pat Schroeder, Democrat, in a speech on women's rights

The trouble with political jokes is that very often they get elected.

Will Rogers

He told us he was going to take crime out of the streets. He did. He took it into the damn White House.

Ralph Abernathy, head of the NAACP, on Richard Nixon

If you took the brains of the majority of the Supreme Court and put them into the head of a bird, the bird would fly backward for ever and ever and ever.

Benjamin Hooks, chairman of the NAACP

He's the only man I know who could look at the swimsuit issue of *Sports Illustrated* and complain the bathing suits weren't flame retardant.

James Baker, the then secretary of state, on Democratic presidential candidate Michael Dukakis

As far as Saddam Hussein being a great military strategist, he is neither a strategist nor is he schooled in operational arts. He's not a tactician. He's not a general. He's not a soldier. Other than that, he's a great military man.

General Norman Schwarzkopf

I can still remember the first time I ever heard Hubert Humphrey speak. He was in the second hour of a five-minute talk.

Gerald Ford, on vice president and presidential hopeful Hubert Humphrey

President William Howard Taft: "I have been talking for a quarter of an hour, but there is so much noise, that I can hardly hear myself talk."
Member of troublesome audience: "That's all right, you're not missing anything."

US Senator Chauncey Depew (glancing at Taft's bulging waistline): "I hope, if it is a girl, Mr. Taft will name it for his charming wife."

President William Taft: "If it is a girl, I shall, of course name if for my lovely helpmate of many years. And if it is a boy, I shall claim the father's prerogative and name it Junior. But if, as I suspect, it is only a bag of wind, I shall name it Chauncey Depew."

A shrub.

Ann Richards, onetime Texas governor, on George W. Bush

Sometimes, when I look at my children, I say to myself, "Lilian, you should have stayed a virgin."

Lillian Carter, no doubt thinking of her son Billy Carter

Nobody likes to be called a liar. But to be called a liar by Bill Clinton is really a unique experience.

Ross Perot, presidential candidate

[Evan Mecham] proves that Darwin was wrong.

Bruce Babbit, then Secretary of the Interior,
on the governor of Arizona

They never open their mouths without subtracting from the sum of human knowledge.

Thomas Reed, Speaker of the House of Representatives, on congressmen

He is a man of splendid abilities but utterly corrupt. Like a rotten mackerel by moonlight, he shines and stinks.

> *John Randolph, congressman, on fellow congressman and the then mayor of New York, Edward Livingstone*

Today, the *L.A. Times* accused Arnold Schwarzenegger of groping six women. I'm telling you, this guy is presidential material.

> *David Letterman*

Arnold Schwarzenegger met with President Bush. It's amazing if you think about it. It was the Terminator and the One-Term-inator.

> *David Letterman*

You know the world is going crazy when the best rapper is a white guy, the best golfer is a black guy, the tallest guy in the NBA is Chinese, the Swiss hold the America's Cup, France is accusing the US of arrogance, Germany doesn't want to go to war, and the three most powerful men in America are named Bush, Dick, and Colon.

> *Chris Rock*

Henry Clay, to Congressman Reed: "I would rather be right than be president." Reed's reply: "He doesn't have to worry. He'll never be either."

A treacherous, gutless old ward-heeler who should be put in a bottle and sent out with the Japanese current.

> *Hunter S. Thompson, on the then vice president Hubert Humphrey*

If the Republicans will stop telling lies about the Democrats, we will stop telling
the truth about them.

Adlai Stevenson, Democratic politician

A pithecanthropoid.

President Roosevelt on the then president of Colombia

The Wizard of Ooze.

*John F. Kennedy, on Senator Everett Dirksen, a man famous for
his verbosity*

An overripe banana, yellow outside, squishy inside.

*Anthony Eden, British prime minister, as described by fellow
politician Reginald Paget*

He is not only a bore, but he bores for England.

Malcolm Muggeridge, on Sir Anthony Eden

When Kissinger can get the Nobel Peace Prize, what is there left for satire?

Tom Lehrer, on Henry Kissinger

It's probably a case of when the mouse is away, the cats will play.

Winston Churchill, on Clement Atlee's apparent reluctance to visit Moscow

A modest little person, with much to be modest about.

Winston Churchill, on the Labour leader Clement Atlee

At the vet's with hard pad, no doubt.

> *Harold Wilson, British prime minister, offering his own idea of why a certain*
>> *female journalist, whom he disliked intensely, had not been present at a*
>>> *press briefing*

He brings to the fierce struggle of politics the tepid enthusiasm of a lazy
summer afternoon at a cricket match.

> *Aneurin Bevan, on Clement Atlee, British prime minister*

I remember when I was a child, being taken to the celebrated Barnum's Circus,
which contained an exhibition of freaks and monstrosities, but the exhibit on
the program which I most desired to see was the one described as "The
Boneless Wonder." My parents judged that spectacle would be too revolting
and demoralizing for my young eyes, and I have waited fifty years to see "The
Boneless Wonder" sitting on the Treasury Bench.

> *Winston Churchill, on Ramsay MacDonald, Britain's first*
>> *Labour Prime Minister, in January 1931*

I must remind the Right Honorable Gentleman that a monologue is not
a decision.

> *Clement Atlee, on Winston Churchill*

Winston Churchill

New MP, whispering in the presence of Churchill: "Poor old Winston, he's gaga."
Churchill, turning to the soon-to-be-embarrassed man: "Yes, and he's deaf, too."

As far as I can see, you have used every cliché except "God is love" and "Please
   adjust your dress before leaving."

> *To Anthony Eden, after a particularly long-winded parliamentary*
> *memorandum (Churchill later denied having said this)*

He is a foul-weather friend.

> *On Lord Beaverbrook*

A curious mix of geniality and venom.

> *On Herbert Morrison, Labour statesman*

It is the only time I've ever seen a rat swimming toward a sinking ship.

> *On a fellow Liberal's defection to the Socialist Party in 1920*

Not as nice as he looks.

On the MP Ian Mikardo, who had an unprepossessing appearance

There, but for the grace of God, goes God.

On Sir Stafford Cripps, Labour statesman

Who will relieve me of this Wuthering Height?

On Sir Stafford Cripps

He has all the virtues I dislike and none of the vices I admire.

On Sir Stafford Cripps

He's a sheep in sheep's clothing.

On Ramsay Macdonald (though usually said to have been spoken of Clement Atlee; Churchill claimed much later, apparently, that it was more appropriately applied to Ramsay)

Sir William Joynson-Hicks, MP, to Churchill: "I wish to remind my Right Honorable Friend that I am only expressing my own opinion."
Churchill, in reply: "And I wish to remind the Honorable Member that I am only shaking my own head."

Anonymous Member of Parliament to Churchill: "Must you fall asleep while I'm speaking?"
Churchill's reply: "No, it is purely voluntary."

The Times is speechless and takes three columns to express its speechlessness.

In a speech in Dundee, May 14, 1908

George Bernard Shaw, in a wire to Churchill: "Am reserving two tickets for you for my premiere (of *St. Joan*). Come and bring a friend—if you have one."

Churchill's reply: "Impossible to be present for the first performance. Will attend the second—if there is one."

Lady Astor, to Churchill: "Winston, if you were my husband, I should flavor your coffee with poison."

Churchill's reply: "Madam, if I were your husband, I should drink it."

Vic Oliver (Churchill's son-in-law), to Churchill: "Who, in your opinion, is the greatest statesman you know?"

Churchill's reply: "Benito Mussolini... Mussolini is the only statesman who had the requisite courage to have his son-in-law executed."

Dead birds don't fall out of their nests.

To the individual in the House of Commons who had (helpfully)
informed Winston that his fly-buttons were undone

Anonymous woman, to Churchill: "There are two things I don't like about you, Mr Churchill—your politics and your moustache."

Churchill's reply: "My dear madam, pray do not disturb yourself. You are not likely to come into contact with either."

Poets

Half song-thrush, half alligator.

Ralph Waldo Emerson, on Walt Whitman

[He] kept one eye on a daffodil and the other on a canal-share.

Walter Savage Landor, on the poet William Wordsworth,
famous for the "golden daffodils" verses

The jingle man.

Ralph Waldo Emerson, on Edgar Allan Poe

Paradise Lost is one of the books which the reader admires and lays down, and
forgets to take up again. Its perusal is a duty rather than pleasure.

Samuel Johnson, on John Milton's epic poem

To see him fumbling with our rich and delicate language is to experience all the
horror of seeing a Sevres vase in the hands of a chimpanzee.

Evelyn Waugh, on Stephen Spender, The Tablet, *May 5, 1951*

Indeed, the whole of Milton's poem is such barbarous trash, so outrageously
offensive to reason and to common sense that one is naturally led to wonder
how it can have been tolerated by a people, among whom astronomy,
navigation, and chemistry are understood.

William Cobbett, on John Milton's epic poem Paradise Lost

If its length be not considered a merit, it hath no other.

Edmund Waller, 17th-century poet, on John Milton's
epic poem Paradise Lost

This obscure, eccentric, and disgusting poem.

Voltaire, on John Milton's epic poem Paradise Lost

Our language sunk under him.

Joseph Addison, on John Milton

Two wiseacres and a cow.

Noël Coward, on English trio Osbert, Sacheverell, and Edith Sitwell

...no jaws nor lips; [the] face of a cock.

Thomas Carlyle, on Ralph Waldo Emmerson

This awful Whitman. This post-mortem poet. This poet with the private soul
leaking out of him all the time. All his privacy leaking out in a sort of dribble,
oozing into the universe.

D. H. Lawrence, on Walt Whitman

...the insuperable proclivity to gin, in poor Lamb. His talk contemptibly small, indicating wondrous ignorance and shallowness, even when it was serious and good-mannered, which it seldom was...ghastly make-believe of wit; in fact, more like "diluted insanity."

Thomas Carlyle, on his contemporary Charles Lamb

Every drop of blood in that man's veins has eyes that look downward.

Ralph Waldo Emerson, on Daniel Webster, American politician

His verse... is the beads without the string.

Gerard Manley Hopkins, on Robert Browning

The world is rid of him, but the deadly slime of his touch remains.

John Constable, on the death of Lord Byron

It is clear, then, nothing is wanting but the mind.

Charles Lamb, on hearing that the poet William Wordsworth felt more than up to the task of writing like Shakespeare, "if he had a mind to try it."

A nice, acrid, savage, pathetic old chap.

I. A. Richards, on Robert Frost, American poet

Mrs. Browning's death is rather a relief to me, I must say. No more Aurora Leighs, thank God!

Edward Fitzgerald, British poet, on Elizabeth Barrett Browning

...there's nothing lost in Og,

    For ever'y inch that is not fool is rogue;

    A monstrous mass of foul corrupted matter,

    As all the devils had spewed to make the batter.

    When wine has given him courage to blaspheme,

    He curses God, but God before curs'd him.

> *English poet John Dryden, on his fellow poet Thomas Shadwell—*
> *whom he renamed Og for the benefit of this particular tirade*

A huge pendulum attached to a small clock.

> *Ivan Panin, on Samuel Taylor Coleridge*

Mr [T. S.] Eliot is at times an excellent poet and has arrived at the supreme
    eminence among English critics largely through disguising himself as
    a corpse.

> *Ezra Pound, American poet, on US-born T. S. Eliot*

A weak, diffusive, weltering, ineffectual man... a great possibility that has not
    realized itself. Never did I see such apparatus got ready for thinking and so
    little thought.

> *Thomas Carlyle, on Samuel Taylor Coleridge*

His imagination resembled the wings of an ostrich. It enabled him to run,
    though not to soar.

> *Thomas Babington Macaulay, about John Dryden*

A half-cracked poetess.

>> *Thomas Wentworth Higginson, of the* Atlantic Monthly, *on the poems of Emily Dickinson, in 1858, when she first sent in her poems to him*

On Waterloo's ensanguined plain
  Lie tens of thousands by him slain;
  But none, by sabre or by shot,
  Fell half so flat as Walter Scott

>> *Thomas, Lord Erskine, in a poetic attack on Sir Walter Scott's poem* The Field of Waterloo

Then Edith Sitwell appeared, her nose longer than an anteater's, and read some
  of her absurd stuff.

>> *Lytton Strachey, English essayist, on Dame Edith Sitwell*

I am debarred from putting her in her place—she hasn't got one.

>> *Dame Edith Sitwell, on an unknown female target*

Sir, he was dull in company, dull in his closet, dull everywhere. He was dull in a
  new way, and that made many people think him GREAT. He was a
  mechanical poet.

>> *Dr. Samuel Johnson, on the poet Thomas Gray*

He walked as if he had fouled his small clothes and looks as if he smelt it.

>> *Christopher Smart, on fellow English poet Thomas Gray*

The opening line contains too many Rs.

Rejection note from a publisher to the poet Ezra Pound, 1912,
for Portrait d'Une Femme

Very nice, though there are dull stretches.

Antoine de Rivarol, commenting on a two-line poem

Bulwer-Lytton I detest. He is the very pimple of the age's humbug.

Nathaniel Hawthorne, on Edward Bulwer-Lytton,
English novelist and dandy

One of the seven humbugs of Xtiandom.

William Morris, English craftsman, on Ralph Waldo Emerson

I am fairly unrepentant about her poetry. I really think that three-quarters of it is gibberish. However, I must crush down these thoughts, otherwise the dove of peace will s**t on me.

Noël Coward, on Dame Edith Sitwell

He is conscious of being decrepit and forgetful, but not of being a bore.

Evelyn Waugh, on Hillaire Belloc

We do not think we could sell a book of his poetry, in fact, we even fear its publication might retard his popularity.

Rejection note from a publisher to George Santayana, 1922

No thanks to: Farrar & Rinehart, Simon & Shuster, Coward-McCann, Limited
Editions, Harcourt, Brace, Random House, Equinox Press, Smith & Haas,
Viking Press, Knopf, Dutton, Harper's, Scribners, Covici, Friede.

Dedication printed in a book by the poet e e cummings
(to all the publishers who had rejected it…)

I am relieved to find the critics shrink from saying that Mr. Yeats will ever be a
popular author. I should really at last despair of mankind, if he could be… The
work does not please the ear, nor kindle the imagination, nor hint a thought
for one's reflection… Do what I will, I can see no sense in the thing: it is to me
sheer nonsense. I do not say it is obscure, or uncouth or barbaric or affected—
tho' it is all these evil things; I say it is to me absolute nullity… I would not
read a page of it again for worlds.

Rejection letter from a publisher, in 1895, to the poet
William Butler Yeats

You are a nasty little man, as well as a third-rate little man. You are impertinent
to your superiors.

Edith Sitwell, English poet, urging her brother Osbert to write a
letter beginning in this way to the society photographer
Cecil Beaton, with whom Osbert had fallen out

[He looks like] an umbrella left behind at a picnic.

George Moore, on William Butler Yeats

In places, this book is a little over-written because Mr. Blunden is no more able
to resist a quotation than some people are to refuse a drink.

George Orwell, on a volume by the poet Edmund Blunden

A face like a wedding-cake left out in the rain.

Anon. (though sometimes attributed to Stephen Spender),
on the visage of the poet W. H. Auden

A tadpole of the Lakes.

Lord Byron, on fellow poet John Keats

Mad, bad, and dangerous to know.

Lady Caroline Lamb, English aristocrat, on Lord Byron, in a diary entry, 1812

In his endeavors to corrupt my mind he has sought to make me smile first at
Vice, saying "There is nothing to which a woman may not be reconciled by
repetition and familiarity." There is no vice with which he has not endeavored
in this manner to familiarize me.

Annabella Milbanke, Lady Byron, on her husband Lord Byron

Of all the bitches alive or dead, a scribbling woman is the most canine.

Lord Byron, on Anna Seward, renowned English poet of the day

A large shaggy dog unchained scouring the beaches of the world and baying at
the moon.

Robert Louis Stevenson, on Walt Whitman

Here are Johnny Keats's piss-a-bed poetry, and three novels by God knows
whom... No more Keats, I entreat: flay him alive; if some of you don't I must
skin him myself: there is no bearing the drivelling idiotism of the Mankin.

Lord Byron, on fellow poet John Keats, in a letter to John Murray, 1818

Fricassee of dead dog... A truly unwise little book.

Thomas Carlyle on Monckton Milnes's Life of Keats

The Sitwells belong to the history of publicity rather than of poetry.

F. R. Leavis, British literary critic, on the Sitwell trio

I spent the morning with the Young-and Pretty-Married Woman, with a skin-like-
a-magnolia-flower... So if this letter should prove dull, well, you will
understand why; for she has sucked my brains as your grandmother was
taught to suck eggs, and the result is that vacuum abhorred by nature.

Dame Edith Sitwell, in a letter to her brother Sacheverell Sitwell, 1916

Talking of poets, I went to a depressing evening where all the guests were
female poets... I met an appalling woman called Madeleine Caron Rock,
extremely fat and exuding a glutinous hysteria from every pore.

Edith Sitwell, English poet, in a letter to fellow poet
Robert Nichols, 1919

He is all ice and wooden-faced acrobatics.

Percy Wyndham Lewis, poet and painter, about W. H. Auden

T. S. Eliot and I like to play, but I like to play euchre, while he likes to play Eucharist.

Robert Frost, on T. S. Eliot

Longfellow is to poetry what the barrel organ is to music.

Van Wyck Brooks, American critic, on Henry Wadsworth Longfellow

There are two ways of disliking poetry; one way is to dislike it, the other is to read Pope.

Oscar Wilde, on Alexander Pope

Some call Pope little nightingale—all sound and no sense.

Lady Mary Wortley Montagu, English woman of letters,
on Alexander Pope

Wordsworth, a stupid man, with a decided gift for portraying nature in vignettes, never yet ruined anyone's morals, unless, perhaps, he has driven some susceptible persons to crime in a very fury of boredom.

Ezra Pound, on William Wordsworth, in Future September

A constipated swan.

Alfred de Musset, on French poet Alfred de Vigny

He hardly drank tea without a stratagem.

Dr. Samuel Johnson, on Alexander Pope

I don't think Robert Browning was very good in bed. His wife probably
didn't care for him very much. He snored and had fantasies about twelve-
year-old girls.

W. H. Auden, on Robert Browning

He was humane but not human.

e e cummings, on Ezra Pound

A village explainer, excellent if you were a village, but if you were not, not.

Gertrude Stein, on Ezra Pound

To me Pound remains the exquisite showman without the show.

Ben Hecht, dramatist, on Ezra Pound

Sir, there is no settling the point of precedency between a louse and a flea.

Dr. Johnson, when asked to rate the relative merits of the poets
Samuel Derrick and Christopher Smart

An old half-witted sheep.

J. K. Stephen, on William Wordsworth

Thou eunuch of language, thou pimp of gender, murderous accoucheur of infant
learning, thou pickle-herring in the puppet show of nonsense.

Robert Burns, Scottish poet, to a critic

A lewd vegetarian.

> *Charles Kingsley, clergyman and author of* The Water Babies, *on poet*
> *Percy Bysshe Shelley*

Tennyson is a beautiful half of a poet.

> *Ralph Waldo Emerson, on Tennyson*

Is Wordsworth a bell with a wooden tongue?

> *Ralph Waldo Emerson, on William Wordsworth*

The best answer to this twaddle is *cui bono?*—a very little Latin phrase very generally mistranslated and misunderstood—*cui bono?*—to whom is it a benefit? If not to Mr. Emerson individually, then surely to no man.

> *Edgar Allan Poe, on Ralph Waldo Emerson, in his* Autobiography

I don't. The Queen does.

> *Dame Edith Sitwell, when asked on a trip to America why she*
> *called herself "Dame"*

So you've been reviewing Edith Sitwell's latest piece of virgin dung, have you? Isn't she a poisonous thing of a woman, lying, concealing, flipping, plagiarizing, misquoting, and being as clever a crooked literary publicist as ever.

> *Dylan Thomas, Welsh poet, on Dame Edith Sitwell*

Dank, limber verses, stuft with lakeside sedges,

And propt with rotten stakes from rotten hedges.

Walter Savage Landor, on William Wordsworth

A dirty man with opium-glazed eyes and rat-taily hair.

Lady Frederick Cavendish, on Tennyson

A louse in the locks of literature.

Tennyson, on the critic Churton Collins

Emerson is one who lives instinctively on ambrosia—and leaves everything

   indigestible on his plate.

Friedrich Nietzsche, German philosopher, on Ralph Waldo Emerson

A poor creature, who has said or done nothing worth a serious man taking the

   trouble of remembering.

Thomas Carlyle, on Percy Bysshe Shelley

Pale, marmoreal Eliot was there last week, like a chapped office boy on a high

   stool, with a cold in his head.

Virginia Woolf, on T. S. Eliot

A hyena that wrote poetry in tombs.

Friedrich Nietzsche, on the Italian poet Dante Alighieri,

famous for his Inferno

Art

Who among us has not gazed thoughtfully and patiently at a painting of
Jackson Pollock and thought, "What a piece of crap?"

Rob Long, critic, in the Modern Review, *1992*

Certainly no man or woman of normal mental health would be attracted by the
sadistic, obscene deformations of Cézanne, Modigliani, Matisse, Gauguin,
and the other Fauves.

John Hemming Fry, art critic, in The Revolt Against Beauty, *1934*

A bunch of lunatics and a woman.

One contemporary critic dismissing the Impressionists
in 1874, the year of their first independent group show
(the woman in question was Berthe Morisot)

Impressions! ...Wallpaper in its embryonic state is more finished!

Louis Leroy, a contemporary critic, dismissing the Impressionists in 1874

My God, they've shot the wrong person!

> *James Pryde, Royal Academician, at the unveiling of a statue to*
> *the nurse Edith Cavell, who was shot as a spy by the Germans in*
> *World War I—he judged the monument to be a poor likeness*

Pretentious, self-indulgent, craftless tat.

> *Ivan Massow, the then chairman of the British Institute of*
> *Contemporary Arts, attacking conceptual art in the*
> New Statesman *magazine, January 2002*

The best view of London is from the National Theatre, because from there you can't see the National Theatre.

> *Anon., reprising Oscar Wilde's famous criticism of the Eiffel*
> *Tower in Paris*

No, we can't just let everyone come.

> *Snub to Ivan Massow, the then chairman of the British Institute*
> *of Contemporary Arts, when his secretary requested a ticket for*
> *him to attend the grand opening of Tate Modern in 2000*

Nazi ambassador in Paris, to Pablo Picasso, on seeing his painting *Guernica* (it depicts the Nazi bombing of the Spanish town): "Oh, it was you, Monsieur Picasso, who did that?"

Picasso's reply: "No, it was you."

A mad German sugar baker dancing naked in a conflagration of his own treacle.

Anon, on Sir Thomas Lawrence's painting
Satan Summoning up his Legions

Try to make Monsieur Pissarro understand that trees are not violet; that the sky is not the color of fresh butter...and that no sensible human being could countenance such aberrations... try to explain to Monsieur Renoir that the torso of a woman is not a mass of decomposing flesh, its green and violet spots indicating the state of complete putrefaction of a corpse.

Albert Wolff, principal art critic of the French newspaper Le Figaro, *on French Impressionist painters Camille Pissarro and Pierre-Auguste Renoir*

These so-called artists style themselves Intransigeants, Impressionists... they throw a few colors on the canvas at random, and then they sign the lot.

Albert Wolff, on the Impressionists, quoted in R.J. Boyle's book American Impressionism, *1974*

A tiny Vulcan with pince-nez, [and] a little twin-pouched bag in which he stuck his poor legs.

Jules Renard, French critic, on Henri Toulouse-Lautrec

M. Cézanne must be some kind of lunatic afflicted with *delirium tremens* when he is painting. In fact, it is one of the weird shapes, thrown off by hashish, borrowed from a swarm of ridiculous dreams.

Anonymous French critic, on Paul Cézanne

Rude enquirer (to James Whistler): "Whatever possessed you to be born in a
   place like Lowell, Massachusetts?"
James Whistler's reply: "I wished to be near my mother."

Come again when you can't stay so long.

Walter Sickert, English painter, bidding farewell to Denton Welch

A buffalo in wolf's clothing.

Robert Ross, on the artist Percy Wyndham Lewis

She has the smile of a woman who has just dined off her husband.

Lawrence Durrell, on the famous Mona Lisa *by Leonardo da Vinci*

[Paul Klee's] pictures seem to resemble not pictures but a sample book of
   patterns of linoleum.

Cyril Asquith, British critic

The only genius with an IQ of 60.

Gore Vidal, on Andy Warhol

Frederic Leighton, to James Whistler: "My dear Whistler, you leave your
   pictures in such a sketchy, unfinished state. Why don't you ever finish them?"
James Whistler's reply: "My dear Leighton, why do you ever begin yours?"

I never saw anything so impudent on the walls of any exhibition, in any country, as last year in London. It was a daub professing to be a "harmony in pink and white" (or some such nonsense); absolute rubbish, and which had taken about a quarter of an hour to scrawl or daub—it had no pretence to be called painting. The price asked for it was two hundred and fifty guineas.

John Ruskin, on James Whistler's Symphony in Grey and Green

...a life passed among pictures makes not a painter—else the policeman in the National Gallery might assert himself. As well allege that he who lives in a library must needs die a poet. Let not Mr. Ruskin flatter himself that more education makes the difference between himself and the policeman when both stand gazing in the Gallery.

James Whistler, on John Ruskin, art critic

A decorator tainted with insanity.

Kenyon Cox, American critic, in Harper's Weekly, *on Paul Gauguin, French painter*

Mr. Whistler always spelt art, and we believe still spells it, with a capital "I."

Oscar Wilde, on James Whistler

The only thoroughly original ideas I have ever heard him express have had reference to his own superiority as a painter over painters greater than himself.

Oscar Wilde, on James Whistler

With our James [Whistler] vulgarity begins at home, and should be allowed to
stay there.

> *Oscar Wilde, on James Whistler, in a letter to the* World

As for M. Cézanne, his name will be forever linked with the most memorable
artistic joke of the last fifteen years.

> *Camille Mauclair, French critic, on Paul Cézanne*

Daubaway Weirdsley.

> *The British satirical magazine* Punch, *passing judgment on*
> *Aubrey Beardsley, British illustrator and author*

He will never be anything but a dauber.

> *Titian, on fellow Italian painter Tintoretto*

[Jacob] Epstein is a great sculptor. I wish he would wash, but I believe
Michelangelo never did, so I suppose it is part of the tradition.

> *Ezra Pound, American poet*

He bores me. He ought to have stuck to his flying machines.

> *Auguste Renoir, on Leonardo da Vinci*

A monstrous carbuncle on the face of a much-loved and elegant friend.

> *Prince Charles, in 1984, on the proposed design for the new*
> *Sainsbury Wing of the National Gallery in London*

He is nothing but a peeping Tom, behind the *coulisses* (stage wings) and among
the dressing rooms of ballet dancers, noting only travesties on fallen
womanhood, most disgusting and offensive.

The Churchman magazine, taking the moral high ground
regarding Edgar Degas, French painter

I have been to it and am pleased to find it more odious than I ever dared hope.

Samuel Butler, on an exhibition of paintings by
Dante Gabriel Rossetti in London

I have seen and heard much of Cockney impudence before now; but never
expected to hear a coxcomb ask two hundred guineas for flinging a pot of
paint in the public's face.

John Ruskin, critic, on James Whistler's
The Falling Rocket *(Whistler sued him for libel, but the*
jury in the case awarded him only a farthing in damages)

The last bit of methane left in the intestine of the dead cow that is post-
modernism.

Robert Hughes, critic, on Jeff Koon's Jeff in the position of Adam

I mock thee not, though I by thee am mocked;
Thou call'st me madman, but I call thee blockhead.

William Blake, English poet and painter, on John Flaxman, sculptor

If people dug up remains of this civilization a thousand years hence, and found
Epstein's statues and that man [Havelock] Ellis, they would think we were
just savages.

Doris Lessing, author, on Jacob Epstein, British sculptor

If this is art it must be ostracized as the poets were banished from
Plato's republic.

Robert Ross, British critic, in the Morning Post, *on Vincent
van Gogh*

Vincent van Gogh's mother painted all of his best things. The famous mailed
decapitated ear was a figment of the public relations firm engaged by van
Gogh's dealer.

Roy Blount, Jr.

It makes me look as if I were straining a stool.

*Winston Churchill, on the infamous portrait of him by British
painter Graham Sutherland (Churchill's wife Clementine
loathed the picture—and had it destroyed)*

It resembles a tortoiseshell cat having a fit in a platter of tomatoes.

Mark Twain, on Turner's painting The Slave Ship

Déjeuner sur l'herbe... is a young man's practical joke, a shameful sore not worth
exhibiting in this way.

Louis Etienne, French critic, on the painting by Édouard Manet

Mr Lewis' pictures appeared... to have been painted by a mailed fist in a cotton glove.

Dame Edith Sitwell, British poet, on Percy Wyndham Lewis

Of course we all know that Morris was a wonderful all-round man, but the act of walking round him has always tired me.

Max Beerbohm, English critic and wit, on William Morris, pioneer of the Arts and Crafts movement in decorative arts, in a letter to S. N. Behrman

Rossetti is not a painter. Rossetti is a ladies' maid.

James Whistler, American painter, on Dante Gabriel Rossetti, British poet and painter

Shockingly mad, madder than ever, quite mad.

Horace Walpole, British commentator, on Henry Fuseli, Swiss-born British artist, famous for his scenes of fantastic, imaginary landscapes

The properties of his figures are sometimes such as might be corrected by a common sign painter.

William Hogarth, British painter and engraver, on Antonio Correggio, 16th-century Italian painter

There is nothing on earth more terrible than English music, except English painting.

Heinrich Heine, German poet and essayist

This is not amusing, it is dismaying and disheartening. The other day, someone attributed to me the statement that "the human race was nearing insanity." I never said that but if anyone is trying to convince me that this is "modern art," and that it is representative of our time, I would be obliged to think that statement is true.

Kenyon Cox, American critic, in Harper's Weekly *on*
Henri Matisse's painting The Red Studio

What is art? Prostitution.

Charles Baudelaire, French poet and perennial cynic, author of
Les Fleurs du Mal

Who is this chap? He drinks, he's dirty, and I know there are women in the background.

Lord Montgomery, on the British portrait painter Augustus John

Friend, to James Whistler: "There are only two great painters, you and Velasquez."
Whistler's reply: "Why drag in Velasquez?"

If you were half a man...and you are.

Franklin P. Adams to the vertically challenged Anglo-American
book illustrator Reginald Birch

Abstract art? A product of the untalented sold by the unprincipled to the
utterly bewildered.

Al Capp

You scarcely knew if you were looking at a parcel of nude flesh or a bundle of
laundry.

Jules Claretie, of Édouard Manet's painting Venus et le Chat
(now known as Olympia*), in* Le Figaro *newspaper*

In the foreground of the carpenter's shop is a hideous, wry-necked, blubbering,
red-haired boy in a night-gown, who appears to have received a poke playing
in an adjacent gutter, and to be holding it up for the contemplation of a
kneeling woman, so horrible in her ugliness that (supposing it were possible
for any human creature to exist for a moment with that dislocated throat) she
would stand out from the rest of the company as a monster in the vilest
cabaret in France or the lowest gin-shop in England.

Charles Dickens, on Millais' painting Christ in the House of His Parents

It looks like a typewriter full of oyster shells; like a broken Pyrex casserole dish
in a brown cardboard box.

Clive James, Australian-born critic, on the Sydney Opera House

In my experience, if you have to keep the lavatory door shut by extending your
left leg, it's modern architecture.

Nancy Banks-Smith

Oscar Wilde

" "

He gets invited to all the Great Houses of England—once.

About Frank Harris

Actress (self deprecatingly) to Oscar Wilde: "Mr. Wilde, you are looking at the ugliest woman in Paris."

Wilde, in a flattering tone: "In the *world*, madam."

Tell the cook of this restaurant with my compliments that these are the very worst sandwiches in the whole world, and that, when I ask for a watercress sandwich, I do not mean a loaf with a field in the middle of it.

In a restaurant

To my regret, I shall have to decline your invitation because of a subsequent engagement.

To an importunate individual

As one turns over the pages the suspense of the author becomes almost
   unbearable.

The Decay of Lying

James Whistler, to Oscar Wilde: "I went past your house this afternoon."
Wilde's response: "Thank you."

Wordsworth went to the lakes, but he never was a lake poet. He found in stones
   the sermons he had already hidden there.

On Romantic poet William Wordsworth

Mr. Marion Crawford has immolated himself upon the altar of local color... he
   has fallen into a bad habit of uttering moral platitudes. He is always telling us
   that to be good is to be good, and that to be bad is to be wicked. At times he
   is almost edifying.

The Decay of Lying

She has exquisite feet and hands, is always *bien chaussée* et *bien gantée*,
   and can talk brilliantly upon any subject, provided that she knows nothing
   about it.

The American Invasion

...A dowdy girl, with one of those characteristic British faces, that, once seen,
   are never remembered.

The Picture of Dorian Gray

A perfect saint among women, but so dreadfully dowdy that she reminded me
of a badly bound hymnbook.

The Picture of Dorian Gray

I never saw anybody take so long to dress, and with such little result.

The Importance of Being Earnest

To Australia? Oh don't mention that dreadful vulgar place.

Lady Windermere's Fan

Many a woman has a past, but I am told that she has at least a dozen, and that
they all fit.

Lady Windermere's Fan

For the British cook is a foolish woman, who should be turned, for all her
inequities, into a pillar of salt which she never knows how to use.

Dinners and Dishes

She wore far too much rouge last night, and not quite enough clothes. That is
always a sign of despair in a woman.

An Ideal Husband

She is a peacock in everything but beauty.

The Picture of Dorian Gray

It is a consolation to know, however, that such an artist as Madame Bernhardt
has not only worn that yellow, ugly dress, but has been photographed in it.

Impressions of America

You should study the peerage, Gerald. It is the one book a young man about
town should know thoroughly, and it is the best thing in fiction the English
has ever done.

A Woman of No Importance

Last night, at Prince's Hall, Mr. Whistler made his first public performance as a
lecturer on art, and spoke for more than an hour with really marvellous
eloquence on the absolute uselessness of all lectures of the kind.

Mr. Whistler's Ten O'Clock

Lewis Morris: "It is a conspiracy of silence against me, a conspiracy of silence.
What should I do?"
Wilde: "Join it."

To be born, or at any rate bred, in a handbag, whether it had handles or not,
seems to me to display a contempt for the ordinary decencies of family life
that reminds one of the worst excesses of the French Revolution.

The Importance of Being Earnest

Mr. James Payn is an adept in the art of concealing what is not worth finding.
He hunts down the obvious with the enthusiasm of a short-sighted detective.

The Decay of Lying

Music

All Bach's last movements are like the running of a sewing machine.

Arnold Bax, on Johan Sebastian Bach

Slavic March—One feels that the composer must have made a bet, for all his
professional reputation was worth, that he would write the most hideous
thing that had ever been put on paper, and he won it, too.

Boston Evening Transcript, *about Tchaikovsky, 1883*

Well, I only hope he saved some of my money to pay for his funeral.

Maria Callas, opera singer, on hearing of the death of her agent

It would kill a cat and turn rocks into scrambled eggs.

Richard Strauss on Wagner's opera Ziegfried

She would be like Richard Wagner if only she looked a bit more feminine.

Osbert Sitwell, poet and writer, on Dame Ethel Smyth

Beautiful, my dear Mozart, but too many notes.

> *Emperor Joseph II (something of a musical dilettante), giving the*
> *benefit of his musical "advice" to Mozart after a performance*
> *of the opera* The Abduction from the Seraglio

It is quite untrue that British people don't appreciate music. They may not
understand it but they absolutely love the noise it makes.

> *Sir Thomas Beecham*

Mr. Adams has done for the arpeggio what McDonalds did for the hamburger.

> The New York Times *on the composer John Adams*

I love Wagner, but the music I prefer is that of a cat hung by its tail outside a
window and trying to stick to the panes of glass with its claws.

> *Charles Baudelaire, the French poet and author, on composer*
> *Richard Wagner*

Is Wagner a human being at all? Is he not rather a disease? Everything he
touches falls ill: he has made music sick

> *Friedrich Nietzsche, on Richard Wagner*

Wagner has beautiful moments but awful quarters of an hour.

> *Gioacchino Rossini, in a letter to Émile Naumann, April 1867*

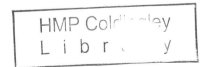

Wagner was a monster. He was anti-Semitic on Mondays and vegetarian on Tuesdays. On Wednesday he was in favor of annexing Newfoundland, Thursday he wanted to sink Venice, and Friday he wanted to blow up the pope.

Tony Palmer, on Richard Wagner

Of all the bête, clumsy, blundering, boggling, baboon-blooded stuff that I ever saw on a human stage, that last night beat—as far as the story and acting went—all the affected, sapless, soulless, beginningless, endless, topless, bottomless, topsiturviest, tuneless, scrabble-pipiest-tongs, and boniest-doggerel of sounds I ever endured the deadliness of, that eternity of nothing was deadliest, as far as its sound went.

John Ruskin, on Richard Wagner

Wagner's music is better than it sounds.

Mark Twain

I like Wagner's music better than any other music. It is so loud that one can talk the whole time without people hearing what one says. That is a great advantage.

Oscar Wilde, on Richard Wagner

I liked your opera. One day I think I'll set it to music.

Richard Wagner, to an aspiring composer; also attributed to
Ludwig van Beethoven

Listening to the Fifth Symphony of Ralph Vaughan Williams is like staring at a
cow for forty-five minutes.

Aaron Copland

Dear, play something you know.

*Elderly (and presumably tone-deaf) woman to child prodigy
Mischa Elman, then aged just seven, who had just completed a
violin recital which he had rounded off with a note-perfect
rendition of Beethoven's* Kreutser *sonata*

I liked the bit about quarter to eleven.

Erik Satie, on From Dawn to Noon on the Sea *from*
La Mer *by Claude Debussy*

I had no idea Stravinsky disliked Debussy as much as this.

Sir Ernest Newman, on Igor Stravinsky's
Symphony of Wind Instruments *in memory of Debussy*

His music used to be original. Now it's aboriginal.

Sir Ernest Newman on Igor Stravinsky

If Beethoven's *Seventh Symphony* is not by some means abridged, it will soon
fall into disuse.

Philip Hale, Boston music critic, in 1837

Beethoven's last quartets were written by a deaf man and should only be listened to by a deaf man.

Sir Thomas Beecham, on Ludwig van Beethoven

The kind of opera that starts at six o'clock and after it has been going three hours you look at your watch and it says 6.20.

David Randolph, on Wagner's opera Parsifal

The Liszt's bombast is bad; it is very bad; in fact there is only one thing worse in his music, and that is his affected and false simplicity. It was said of George Sand (the French author) that she had a habit of speaking and writing concerning chastity in such terms that the very word became impure; so it is with the simplicity of Liszt.

Philip Hale, Boston music critic, on Franz Liszt

Composition, indeed! Decomposition is the word for such hateful fungi.

Dramatic and Musical World of 1855, *on Franz Liszt*

Music makes one feel so romantic, at least it always gets on one's nerves which is the same thing nowadays.

Oscar Wilde

No opera plot can be sensible, for people do not sing when they are feeling sensible.

W. H. Auden

Music is the brandy of the damned.

George Bernard Shaw

Anything too stupid to be said is sung.

Voltaire

Tell me, George, if you had to do it all over, would you fall in love with yourself
again?

Oscar Levant, noted wit, to composer George Gerswhin

Oscar, why don't you sit down and play us a medley of your hit?

George Gershwin, composer, to fellow composer
Oscar Levant

Leonard Bernstein has been disclosing musical secrets that have been well
known for over four hundred years.

Oscar Levant

Fritz Kreisler, violinist (to Mrs. Cornelius Vanderbilt, wealthy socialite): "My fee
[to play at your party] is $18,000 dollars."
Mrs. Cornelius Vanderbilt's reply: "That's agreeable, but I hope you understand
that you should not mingle with my guests."
Fritz Kreisler's reply: "Oh! Well, in that case, my fee is only $500."

The prelude to [Wagner's] *Tristan und Isolde* reminds one of the old Italian painting of a martyr whose intestines are slowly unwound from his body on a reel.

Eduard Hanslick

It gives us, for the first time, the hideous notion that there can be music which stinks to the ear.

Eduard Hanslick, on Tchaikovsky's Violin Concerto

A tub of pork and beer.

Hector Berlioz, composer, on fellow composer George F. Handel

Handel is only fourth rate. He is not even interesting.

Peter Ilich Tchaikovsky, on George F. Handel

...nothing but the caperings and gibberings of a big baboon, over-excited by a dose of alcoholic stimulus.

George Templeton Strong, British critic, on Le Carnival Romain
by Hector Berlioz in a diary entry

Berlioz, musically speaking, is a lunatic; a classical composer only in Paris, the great city of quacks. His music is simply and undisguisedly nonsense.

The Dramatic and Musical Review of 1843, *on Hector Berlioz*

If he'd been making shell cases during the [First World] war it might have been
better for music.

> *Camille Saint-Saëns, on fellow French composer Maurice Ravel*

Liszt's orchestral music is an insult to art. It is gaudy musical harlotry, savage
and incoherent bellowings.

> The Boston Gazette, *on Franz Liszt*

It's bad when they don't perform your operas—but when they do, it's far worse.

> *Camille Saint-Saens, to Dame Ethel Smyth, composer*

Debussy played the piano with the lid down.

> *Robert Bresson, on Claude Debussy*

Oh you arch-ass—you double-barrelled ass!

> *Ludwig van Beethoven on Gottfried Weber, music critic*

Beethoven always sounds like the upsetting of bags—with here and there a
dropped hammer.

> *John Ruskin, British critic*

Rossini would have been a great composer if his teacher had spanked him
enough on his backside.

> *Ludwig van Beethoven*

After Rossini dies, who will be there to promote his music?

Richard Wagner, on Gioacchino Rossini

One can't judge Wagner's opera *Lohengrin* after a first hearing, and I certainly
don't intend hearing it a second time.

Gioacchino Rossini, on Richard Wagner

Woman rail passenger, lighting a cigarette: "You won't object if I smoke?"
Sir Thomas Beecham: "Certainly not—and you won't object if I'm sick."
Woman rail passenger (crossly): "I don't think you know who I am; I am one of
the [railway] director's wives."
Sir Thomas Beecham: "Madam, if you were the director's only wife, I should
be sick."

Jazz: Music invented for the torture of imbeciles.

Henry van Dyke

Perhaps it was because Nero played the fiddle, they burned Rome.

Oliver Herford

Rachmaninov's immortalizing totality was his scowl. He was a six-and-a-half
foot scowl.

Igor Stravinsky, Russian composer, on fellow Russian composer
Sergei Rachmaninov

Shostakovich is without doubt the foremost composer of pornographic music in the history of art.

W. J. Henderson, music critic, on Dmitri Shostakovich

Splitting the convulsively inflated larynx of the Muse, Berg utters tortured mistuned cackling, a pandemonium of chopped-up orchestral sounds, mishandled men's throats, bestial outcries, bellowing, rattling, and all other evil noises... Berg is the poisoner of the well of German music.

Germania, on Alban Berg, Austrian composer

The audience seemed rather disappointed; they expected the ocean, something big, something colossal, but they were served instead with some agitated water in a saucer.

Louis Schneider, on La Mer *by Claude Debussy*

The musical equivalent of blancmange.

Bernard Levin, British journalist, on Frederick Delius, British composer

The singers and crew are not only useless in themselves but spread about at large their contagious effeminacy.

William Cobbett, English journalist, agricultural reformer, and radical politician, on Italian singers in London

The musical equivalent of St. Pancras station.

Sir Thomas Beecham on Edward Elgar's Symphony in A Flat

What a giftless b*****d! It annoys me that this self-inflated mediocrity is hailed
as a genius. Why, in comparison with him, Raff is a giant, not to speak of
Rubinstein, who is after all a live and important human being, while Brahms
is chaotic and absolutely empty dried-up stuff.

Peter Tchaikovsky, on German composer Johannes Brahms,

in his diary, 1886

There are some experiences in life which should not be demanded twice from
any man, and one of them is listening to the *Brahms Requiem.*

George Bernard Shaw

If you will make a point of singing "All we, like sheep, have gone astray" with a
little less satisfaction, we shall meet the aesthetical as well as the theological
requirements.

Sir Thomas Beecham, to a choir he was conducting

We can't expect you to be with us all the time, but perhaps you would be good
enough to keep in touch now and again.

Sir Thomas Beecham, to a player in the orchestra he was conducting

Oh well, you play Bach your way; I'll play him his.

Harpsichordist Wanda Landowska to a fellow musician

What, nothing from Mozart?

Sir Thomas Beecham, on the many greetings he was receiving in

honor of his 70th birthday

I am not the greatest conductor in this country. On the other hand, I'm better
than any damned foreigner.

Sir Thomas Beecham

A glorified bandmaster!

Sir Thomas Beecham, on the Italian conductor Arturo Toscanini

The sound of a harpsichord—two skeletons copulating on a tin roof in a
thunderstorm.

Sir Thomas Beecham

He reeks of Horlicks.

Sir Thomas Beecham, on conductor Sir Adrian Boult

Please do not shoot the pianist. He is doing his best.

Oscar Wilde, in Impressions of America

The funeral dirge of a fried eel.

George Bernard Shaw, on the socialist anthem The Red Flag

No, but I've stepped in it.

Sir Thomas Beecham, asked whether he had played any Stockhausen

The chief objection to playing wind instruments is that it prolongs the life of
the player.

George Bernard Shaw

Miss Truman is a unique American phenomenon with a pleasant voice of little
size and fair quality... yet Miss Truman cannot sing very well. She is flat a
good deal of the time... she communicates almost nothing of the music she
presents... There are few moments during her recital when one can relax, and
feel confident that she will make her goal, which is the end of her song.

Paul Hume, of the Washington Post, *on a recital by*
Margaret Truman in 1950

[Like] piddling on flannel.

Noel Coward, on the music of Mozart

I don't mind what language an opera is sung in so long as it is a language I don't
understand.

Sir Edward Appleton

Difficult do you call it, Sir? I wish it were impossible.

Dr. Samuel Johnson, on hearing a famous violinist

Brass bands are all very well in their place; outdoors and several miles away.

Sir Thomas Beecham

I didn't know that he'd been knighted. It was only yesterday he was doctored.

Sir Thomas Beecham, on fellow conductor Sir Malcolm Sargent,
who was awarded a knighthood in the 1947 Honors List

I had not realized the Arabs were so musical.

>*Sir Thomas Beecham, on hearing that a concert in Tel Aviv, conducted by Sir Malcolm Sargent, had been interrupted by the sound of gunfire*

A kind of musical Malcolm Sargent.

>*Sir Thomas Beecham, of the conductor Herbert von Karajan (referring to his longtime rival, Sir Malcolm Sargent)*

She was a singer who had to take any note above A with her eyebrows.

>*Frank Muir, on Montague Glass*

His writing is limited to songs for dead blondes.

>*Keith Richards, about Elton John*

The biggest no-talent I ever worked with.

>*Paul Cohen, on Buddy Holly*

I'm glad I've given up drugs and alcohol. It would be awful to be like Keith Richards. He's pathetic. It's like a monkey with arthritis, trying to go on stage and look young. I have great respect for the Stones but they would have been better if they had thrown Keith out 15 years ago.

>*Elton John, about Keith Richards*

I love his work but I couldn't warm to him even if I was cremated next to him.

>*Keith Richards, about Chuck Berry*

I think Mick Jagger would be astounded and amazed if he realized to how many people he is not a sex symbol but a mother image.

David Bowie

He sings like he's throwing up.

Andrew O'Connor, about Bryan Ferry

Beatlemania is like the frenzied dancing and shouting of voodoo worshippers and the howls and bodily writhings of converts among primitive evangelical sects in the southern states of America.

Dr. F. Casson, British academic, in the Times *newspaper, 1963*

Boy George is all England needs—another queen who can't dress.

Joan Rivers

Michael Jackson was a poor black boy who grew up to be a rich white woman.

Molly Ivins

Michael [Jackson] is claiming racism. And I say... honey, you've got to pick a race first. All of a sudden you're a black man, then you're Diana Ross, now you're Audrey Hepburn. Then he's got the little beard going on. He's like Lord Of The Rings, the entire cast. Michael's about to jump species.

Robin Williams

He hasn't just lost the plot; he's lost the whole library!

Melody Maker, *on Michael Jackson*

Is he just doing a bad Elvis pout, or was he born that way?

Freddie Mercury, on Billy Idol

He sounds like he's got a brick dangling from his willy, and a food-mixer making purée of his tonsils.

Paul Lester, about Jon Bon Jovi

Actually, I never liked Dylan's kind of music before; I always thought he sounded just like Yogi Bear.

Mike Ronson, on Bob Dylan

This deadly, winking, sniggering, snuggling, scent-impregnated, chromium-plated, luminous, quivering, giggling, fruit-flavored, mincing, ice-covered heap of mother love...

Daily Mirror's *journalist William Connor on Liberace in 1956*

I cried all the way to the bank.

Liberace on a bad review

Sleeping with George Michael would be like having sex with a groundhog.

Boy George

Elvis transcends his talent to the point of dispensing with it altogether.

Greil Marcus, on Elvis Presley

Presley sounded like Jayne Mansfield looked—blowsy and loud and low.

Julie Burchill, British journalist, about Elvis Presley

He looks like a dwarf who's been dipped in a bucket of pubic hair.

Boy George, about Prince

Even the deaf would be traumatized by prolonged exposure to the most hideous croak in Western culture. Richards' voice is simply horrible.

Nick Coleman, about Keith Richards

He was so mean it hurt him to go to the bathroom.

Britt Eklund, on Rod Stewart

It's one thing to want to save lives in Ethiopia, but it's another thing to inflict so much torture on the British public.

Morrissey, singer, on Bob Geldof's Band Aid

I was swamped with telephone calls from the British press asking me what I'd do if a Smiths fan went out and shot Maggie (Margaret Thatcher, the then prime minister of Great Britain). "Well," I said, "I'd obviously marry this person."

Morrissey, on the group The Smiths

[Elvis Costello] looks like Buddy Holly after drinking a can of STP Oil Treatment.

Dave Marsh, writer, in Rolling Stone *magazine*

Is it a sausage? It is certainly smooth and damp looking, but whoever heard of a
172lb sausage, six-feet-tall?

Time magazine, on Elvis Presley

Somebody should clip Sting around the head and tell him to stop using that
ridiculous Jamaican accent.

Elvis Costello, on Sting

She's like a breast with a boom box.

Judy Tenuta, comedienne, on Madonna

Bambi with testosterone.

*Owen Glieberman of Entertainment Weekly on
The Artist Formerly Known as Prince*

All legs and hair with a mouth that could swallow the whole stadium and the
hot-dog stand.

Laura Lee Davies, on Tina Turner

Leonard Cohen gives you the feeling that your dog just died.

Review in the British Q magazine

I couldn't stand Janis Joplin's voice. She was just a screaming little
loudmouthed chick.

Arthur Lee, on Janis Joplin

I am amazed at radio DJs today. I am firmly convinced that AM on my radio
stands for Absolute Moron. I will not begin to tell you what FM stands for.

Jasper Carrott, British comedian

She's so hairy when she lifted up her arm I thought it was Tina Turner in her
armpit.

Joan Rivers, on Madonna

If life was fair, Elvis would be alive and all the impersonators would be dead.

Johnny Carson

He moves like a parody between a majorette girl and Fred Astaire.

Truman Capote, on Mick Jagger

Michael Bolton said yesterday he now wants to become an opera singer. Which
is great, because now my Dad and I can hate the same kind of music.

Conan O'Brien

Michael Bolton sounds like he's having his teeth drilled by Helen Keller.

Jeff Wilder

She's about as sexy as a Venetian blind.

Madonna, on Sinead O'Connor

He sang like a hinge.

Ethel Merman, on Cole Porter

I think Robbie Williams is an a**hole. I think he is a very misguided, easily led, stupid, foolish young individual who'd benefit from a slapping. I'd probably kick him down the stairs a couple of times, but I'm not a violent person and I don't like confrontation. His music's s**t too. Apart from that, he's a nice guy.

Noel Gallagher, Oasis lead singer, on Robbie Williams

When they asked Jack Benny to do something for the Actor's Orphanage, he shot both his parents and moved in.

Bob Hope, on Jack Benny

When Jack Benny plays the violin, it sounds as if the strings are still back in the cat.

Fred Allen

Michael Jackson's album was only called "Bad" because there wasn't enough room on the sleeve for "Pathetic."

The Artist Formerly Known as Prince, about Michael Jackson

Bob Geldof is a loss to the road-sweeping profession, as well as actually looking like something swept up.

Jilly Parkin

I was a fan of hers back when she was popular.

Mariah Carey, when asked if she was a fan of Madonna

This is the same country that buys Mariah Carey records. It has nothing to do with art.

Madonna

I look at my friendship with her as like having a gallstone. You deal with it, there is pain, and then you pass it. That's all I have to say about Schmadonna.

Sandra Bernhard, on Madonna

He plays four-and-a-half-hour sets. That's torture. Does he hate his audience?

John Lydon, on Bruce Springsteen

Their lyrics are unrecognizable as the Queen's English.

Edward Heath, British prime minister, on The Beatles

Quite frankly, I've never understood what Mick Jagger saw in that bucktoothed Texas nag. There are a thousand home-grown Texas drag queens who could do Jerry Hall better than she does herself.

Camille Paglia, American feminist writer

With Mick Jagger's lips, he could French-kiss a moose.

Joan Rivers

If I go around to someone's house and there's an Eric Clapton record, I just walk out.

Jon Moss, on Eric Clapton

"If I had a hammer," I'd use it on Peter, Paul, and Mary.

Howard Rosenberg, on the hit song

The sheets of sound they let loose have the cumulative effect of mugging.

The Times *newspaper, on The Clash*

Who's judging American Idol? Paula Abdul? Paula Abdul judging a singing contest is like Christopher Reeve judging a dance contest!

Chris Rock, at the VMA Awards, 2003

She is closer to organized prostitution than anything else.

Morrissey, on Madonna

Her voice sounded like an eagle being goosed.

Ralph Novak, on Yoko Ono

The band is now basically a T-shirt-selling machine. Jumping Jack Flash no more; more like Limping Hack Flash.

Julie Burchill, on The Rolling Stones

A baroque art-rock bubblegum broadcast on a frequency understood only by female teenagers and bred field mice.

Mark Coleman, on Duran Duran

Time to visit the midget.

Madonna, on Prince

Literature

Ah! ...He'd make a lovely corpse.

Sarah Gump, in Charles Dickens' novel Martin Chuzzlewit

Mr. Squeers's appearance was not prepossessing. He had but one eye, and the popular prejudice runs in favour of two.

From Charles Dickens' novel Nicholas Nickleby

She dotes on poetry, sir. She adores it; I may say that her whole soul and mind are wound up, and entwined with it. She has produced some delightful pieces, herself, sir. You may have met with her *Ode to an Expiring Frog*, sir.

Leo Hunter, in Charles Dickens' novel The Pickwick Papers

...Take another glass of wine, and excuse my mentioning that society as a body does not expect one to be so strictly conscientious in emptying one's glass, as to turn it bottom upwards with the rim on one's nose.

Herbert Pocket, in Charles Dickens' novel Great Expectations

Errant, malmsey-nose knave!

Mistress Quickly, Henry IV, Part 2 *by William Shakespeare*

'Sblood, you starveling, you elf-skin, you dried neat's tongue, you bull's pizzle, you stock-fish! O for breath to utter what is like thee! You tailor's-yard, you sheath, you bowcase; you vile standing-tuck,—

Falstaff, to Prince Henry, King Henry IV, Part 1 *by William Shakespeare*

This woman's an easy glove, my lord; she goes off and on at pleasure.

Lafeu, All's Well That Ends Well *by William Shakespeare*

He has not so much brain as earwax.

Thersites, Troilus and Cressida *by William Shakespeare*

Mome, malthorse, capon, coxcomb, idiot, patch!

Dromio of Syracuse, The Comedy of Errors *by William Shakespeare*

Foul words is but foul wind, wind is but foul breath, and foul breath is noisome; therefore I will depart unkissed.

Beatrice to Benedict in Shakespeare's Much Ado About Nothing

The Devil damn thee black, thou cream-fac'd loon!
Where gott'st thou that goose look?

Macbeth, to an attendant in Shakespeare's play of that name

121

Away, you cut-purse rascal! You filthy bung, away! By this wine, I'll thrust my
knife in your mouldy chaps, an you play the saucy cuttle with me. Away, you
bottle-ale rascal! you basket-hilt stale juggler, you!

Doll Tearsheet, Henry IV, Part 2 *by William Shakespeare*

A knave, a rascal, an eater of broken meats; a base, proud, shallow, beggarly,
three-suited, hundred-pound, filthy, worsted-stocking knave; a lily-livered,
action-taking knave; a whoreson, glass-gazing, super-serviceable finical rogue;
a one-trunk-inheriting slave; one that wouldst be a bawd, in way of good
service, and art nothing but the composition of a knave, beggar, coward,
pandar, and the son and heir of a mongrel bitch: one whom I will beat into
clamorous whining, if thou deniest the least syllable of thy addition.

Kent to Oswald, King Lear *by William Shakespeare*

...your virginity, your old virginity, is like one of our French withered pears: it
looks ill, it eats drily; marry, 'tis a withered pear...

Parolles to Helena, All's Well that Ends Well *by William Shakespeare*

No! why art thou then exasperate, thou idle immaterial skein of sleave-silk, thou
green sarcenet flap for a sore eye, thou tassel of a prodigal's purse, thou? Ah,
how the poor world is pestered with such waterflies, diminutives of nature!

Thersites, Troilus and Cressida *by William Shakespeare*

Pish for thee, Iceland dog! thou prick-ear'd cur of Iceland!

Pistol, Henry V *by William Shakespeare*

The kind of man...whom every body speaks well of, and nobody cares about; whom all are delighted to see, and nobody remembers to talk to.

Description of the character Willoughby, in the novel Sense and Sensibility *by Jane Austen*

She looked like a million dollars, I must admit, even if in well-used notes.

Angela Carter, in her novel Wise Children

She's the sort of woman who lives for others—you can always tell the others by their hunted expression.

C.S. Lewis, in his book The Screwtape Letters

Prostitution gives her an opportunity to meet people.

Joseph Heller, in his novel Catch 22

The Right Hon. was a tubby little chap who looked as if he had been poured into his clothes and had forgotten to say "When!"

P.G. Wodehouse, Very Good Jeeves

Waldo is one of those people who would be enormously improved by death.

The short-story writer Saki (pseudonym of H. H. Munro), in The Feast of Nemesis

He had just enough intelligence to open his mouth when he wanted to eat, but certainly no more.

P.G. Wodehouse, Barmy in Wonderland

Eric: "Philippa happens to be very good with children."

Helen: "Presumably why she lives with you."

Exchange from Alan Ayckbourn's play Ten Times Table

Two of the nicest people if ever there was one.

Alan Bennett, on Sidney and Beatrice Webb in his satirical piece
Forty Years On

But if you observe, people always live for ever when there is an annuity to be
paid them.

Mrs. John Dashwood, in the novel Sense and Sensibility *by Jane Austen*

[Mrs. Ferrars] was not a woman of many words; for, unlike people in general,
she proportioned them to the number of her ideas.

Sense and Sensibility, *by Jane Austen*

This is Mr. St. Barbe, who when the public taste has improved, will be the most
popular author of the day. In the meantime, he will give you a copy of his
novel, which has not sold as well as it ought to have done.

Benjamin Disraeli, getting his own back on William Makepeace
Thackeray in his own novel Endymion, *which contains a thinly*
disguised caricature of Thackeray in the character of St. Barbe

Film Scripts

I am big. It's the pictures that got small.

> *Gloria Swanson, in* Sunset Boulevard, *to William Holden who remarked to her, "Didn't you used to be big in pictures?"*

I'd hate to take a bite out of you. You're a cookie full of arsenic.

> *J. J Hunsecker (Burt Lancaster) to Sidney Falco (Tony Curtis), in* Sweet Smell of Success

Your idea of fidelity is not having more than one man in the bed at the same time.

> *Dirk Bogarde to Julie Christie in the movie* Darling

Remember, you're fighting for this woman's honor, which is probably more than she ever did.

> *From the movie Duck Soup*

It's getting late. I was beginning to worry. I was afraid you weren't in
  an accident.

> *Jill Clayburgh to Burt Reynolds in the movie* Starting Over

Laurence Harvey: "Look, Gloria, I have to spend at least tonight with [my wife]."
Elizabeth Taylor: "A good night's sleep will be the best thing for you."

> *From the movie* Butterfield 8

Vivien Leigh: "Rhett, if you go, where shall I go? What shall I do?"
Clark Gable: "Frankly, my dear, I don't give a damn."

> *From the movie* Gone With the Wind

Had I been sterile, darling, I'd be happier today.

> *Katharine Hepburn to Anthony Hopkins, one of her sons, in the*
> *movie* The Lion in Winter

His mother should have thrown him out and kept the stork.

> *Mae West, in the movie* Belle of the Nineties

I see you're a man with ideals. I guess I better be going while you've still
  got them.

> *Mae West, in the movie* My Little Chickadee, *to an honest man*

It's not the men in my life, but the life in my men.

> *Mae West, in the movie* I'm No Angel ,
> *rephrasing a reporter's questions*

Edward Arnold: "I changed my mind."

Mae West: "Does it work any better?"

Edward Arnold and Mae West in the movie I'm No Angel

Full blooded? Quite the antitheses. He's very anemic.

Mae West, in the movie My Little Chickadee,
in response to Mrs. Gideon (Margaret Hamilton) who asks if
Twillie's Native American companion is a full-blooded Indian

Goodness had nothing to do with it, dearie.

Mae West, in response to a hat-check girl who compliments her jewelry
with the exclamation "Goodness! What diamonds!" in the movie Night After
Night. *The line was later used as the title of her autobiography*

Some men are all right in their place–if they only knew the right places.

Mae West, in the movie Klondike Annie

If she has another facelift, she'll be wearing a beard.

Comment made about the actress/singer Cher, in the British TV
series Absolutely Fabulous

Marriage isn't a word...it's a sentence!

From the movie The Crowd

I'd love to kiss you, but I just washed my hair.

Bette Davis, in the movie Cabin in the Cotton

I married your mother because I wanted children. Imagine my disappointment
  when you arrived.

Groucho Marx, in the movie Horse Feathers

"Sir! This lady is my wife. You should be ashamed."
"If this lady is your wife, you should be ashamed."

Exchange in the Groucho Marx movie A Night in Casablanca

Shirley Maclaine: "How is she?"
Doctor: "I always tell people to hope for the best and prepare for the worst."
Shirley Maclaine: "And they let you get away with that?"

From the movie Terms of Endearment

Mr. Allen, this may come as a shock to you, but there are some men who don't
  end every sentence with a proposition.

Doris Day to Rock Hudson in the movie Pillow Talk

Will you take your hands off me? What are you playing, osteopath?

Rosalind Russell to Cary Grant in the movie His Girl Friday

There's a name for you ladies, but it isn't used in high society—outside of
  a kennel.

Joan Crawford, in the movie The Women

You know, you wouldn't be a bad-looking dame... if it wasn't for your face.

From the movie Hold Your Man

That's okay, we can walk to the kerb from here.

Woody Allen, to Diane Keaton in Annie Hall

—referring to her bad parking

Except for socially, you're my role model.

Joan Cusack to Holly Hunter in the movie Broadcast News

I'm not sure she's capable of any real feelings. She's television generation. She
learned life from Bugs Bunny.

William Holden, about Faye Dunaway in the movie Network

If I were the cream for that woman's coffee, I'd curdle.

Kathleeen Howard in the movie Ball of Fire

After one month with you, Mr. Whiteside, I am going to work in a munitions
factory. From now on, anything that I can do to help exterminate the human
race will fill me with the greatest of pleasure. Mr. Whiteside, if Florence
Nightingale had ever nursed you, she would have married Jack the Ripper
instead of founding the Red Cross.

Mary Wickes to Monty Woolley in the movie
The Man Who Came to Dinner

I remember every detail. The Germans wore gray. You wore blue.

Humphrey Bogart in Casablanca

How did you get into that dress—with a spray gun?

>> *Bob Hope to Dorothy Lamour in the movie* Road to Rio

That's quite a dress you almost have on.

>> *Gene Kelly to Nina Foch in the movie* An American in Paris

I've met a lot of hard-boiled eggs in my time, but you are twenty minutes.

>> *Billy Wilder in the movie* Ace in the Hole

I know exactly how you feel, my dear. The morning after always does look grim if you happen to be wearing last night's dress.

>> *Ina Claire to Greta Garbo in the movie* Ninotchka

Good grief! I hate to tell you, dear, but your skin makes the Rocky Mountains look like chiffon velvet!

>> *Salon client, looking through a magnifying glass in the movie* The Women

Doris Black (about Dustin Hoffman in drag): "I'd like to make her look a little more attractive. How far can you pull back?"

Cameraman: "How do you feel about Cleveland?"

>> *From the movie* Tootsie

What God has not given to Antoinette Green, Antoinette Green has had done.

>> *Liza Minnelli in the movie* The Sterile Cuckoo

Funny thing is, you are sort of attractive, in a corn-fed sort of way. I can imagine
some poor girl falling for you if—well, if you threw in a set of dishes.

Bette Davis to Richard Travis in the movie
The Man Who Came to Dinner

He runs four miles a day and has a body like Mark Spitz. Unfortunately, he still
has a face like Ernest Borgnine.

Ellen Burstyn about her husband in the movie Same Time, Next Year

Shandra Berri: "He's got a great ass."
Daryl Hannah: "Too bad it's on his shoulders."

From the movie Roxanne

Jack Nicholson: "I like the lights on."
Shirley Maclaine: "Then go home and turn them on."

From the movie Terms of Endearment

Sometimes when I've got a ballplayer alone, I'll just read Emily Dickinson or
Walt Whitman to him. And the guys are so sweet, they always stay and listen.
Course, a guy'll listen to anything if he thinks it's foreplay.

Susan Sarandon in the movie Bull Durham

I can feel the hot blood pounding through your varicose veins.

Jimmy Durante to Mary Wickes in The Man Who Came to Dinner

Will you take your clammy hands off my chair? You have the touch of a love-starved cobra.

Monty Woolley to Mary Wickes in The Man Who Came to Dinner

If we end up together, then this is the most romantic day of my whole life. And if we don't, then I'm a complete slut.

Kathleen Turner to Michael Douglas in the movie
The War of the Roses

Dean Bastounes (one-night stand): "So what's for breakfast?"
Elizabeth Perkins: "Egg McMuffin. Corner of Broadway and Belmont."

From the movie About Last Night...

Ralph Bellamy (about Cary Grant): "He's not the man for you—I can see that—but I sorta like him. He's got a lot of charm."
Rosalind Russell: "Well, he comes by it naturally. His grandfather was a snake."

From the movie His Girl Friday

Jill Clayburgh: "I understand. It's too much, it's too soon, or you don't like me enough, or you like me too much, or you're frightened or you're guilty, you can't get it up or out or in or what?!"
Burt Reynolds: "That just about covers it."

From the movie Starting Over

Jack Nicholson: "I didn't know anybody old enough, so I thought, well, I'll ask my next-door neighbor. Well, anyway, they canceled the dinner, but I was really thinking about asking you out. Seriously. Isn't that a shocker?"
Shirley Maclaine: "Yes. Imagine you having a date with someone where it wasn't necessarily a felony."

From the movie Terms of Endearment

Martha, in my mind you are buried in cement right up to the neck. No, up to the nose, it's quieter.

Richard Burton to Elizabeth Taylor in the movie Who's Afraid of
Virginia Woolf

Alan Bates: "Do you want to see other men?"
Jill Clayburgh: "Not today."

From the movie An Unmarried Woman

Wait a minute. Wait a minute! Is this a proposal, or are you taking an inventory?

Mae West, in the movie Belle of the Nineties, in response to the
declaration, "I must have your golden hair, fascinating eyes,
alluring smile, your lovely arms, your form divine"

Will you marry me? Did he leave you any money? Answer the second question first.

Groucho Marx, in the movie Duck Soup

The Movies

In a mere half-century films have gone from silent to unspeakable.

Doug Larson

I wouldn't say when you've seen one Western you've seen the lot; but when you've seen the lot you get the feeling you've seen one.

Katherine Whitehorn

I deny I ever said that actors are cattle. What I said was, "Actors should be treated like cattle."

Alfred Hitchcock

Apocalyptic swank...each shot looks like an album cover for records you don't ever want to play.

Movie critic Pauline Kael on Paul Schrader's Cat People

Which part is he playing now?

> *Somerset Maugham, passing comment on the actor*
> *Spencer Tracy during the filming of* Dr. Jekyll and Mr. Hyde

The worst thing that has happened to movies since Lassie played a war veteran
with amnesia.

> *Rex Reed, on Marlon Brando in* The Chase

Wet she was a star, dry she ain't.

> *Joe Pasternak on swimming film star (!) Esther Williams*

Cecil B. De Mille, to Arthur Mayer: "How can you say good pictures lose money?
My pictures are invariably profitable."
Mayer's reply: "But yours are the run of De Mille pictures."

Click, click, click.

> *Katharine Hepburn, referring to the cogs whirring inside the*
> *head of Meryl Streep, her least-favorite actress*

The cruellest thing that has happened to Lincoln since he was shot by Booth
was to fall into the hands of Carl Sandburg.

> *Edmund Wilson, on the TV miniseries*
> *on the life of Abraham Lincoln*

This arrogant, sour, ceremonial, pious, chauvinistic egomaniac.

> *Elliot Gould, on fellow US movie actor Jerry Lewis*

He has Van Gogh's ear for music.

> *Billy Wilder, on actor Cliff Osmond, called upon to sing—for the*
> *first time—in a Wilder movie*

Maybe it's the hair. Maybe it's the teeth. Maybe it's the intellect. No, it's the hair.

> *Tom Shales, on Farrah Fawcett*

The curvaceous Bo Derek comes off as erotically as a Dresden doll.

> The Motion Picture Guide *on the movie* Bolero

Hostess, to British comic actor Leonard Rossiter, as he was leaving a party: "Do
you have to leave so early?"

Rossiter's reply: "No, it's purely a matter of choice."

Working with Julie Andrews was like being hit over the head with a Valentine's
card.

> *Christopher Plummer, on his experience with the actress while filming*
> The Sound of Music

A man of many talents—all of them minor.

> *Leslie Halliwell, critic, of director Blake Edwards*

Anyone might become homosexual after seeing Glenda Jackson naked.

> *Auberon Waugh—doubtless with the film of the*
> *D.H. Lawrence novel,* Women in Love, *in mind*

His life was a fifty-year-old trespass against good taste.

Leslie Mallory, on swashbuckling hero Erroll Flynn

I presume that you also came from a long line of hunchbacks.

George S. Kaufman, to the actor Charles Laughton, who had attributed his
great success as Captain Bligh in the movie Mutiny on the Bounty *to the*
fact that he had come from a seafaring family (Laughton was now playing
Quasimodo, in the movie The Hunchback of Notre Dame...)

You can't direct a Laughton picture. The best you can hope for is to referee.

Alfred Hitchcock, on the actor Charles Laughton

She's one of the few actresses in Hollywood history who looks more animated in
still photographs than she does on the screen.

Michael Medved, on Raquel Welsh

Her work, if that is the word for it, always consists chiefly of a dithering,
blithering, neurotic coming apart at the seams—an acting style that is really a
nervous breakdown in slow motion.

John Simon, on Diane Keaton

He looked like a half-melted rubber bulldog.

John Simon, on Walter Matthau

I have more talent in my smallest fart than you have in your entire body.

Walter Matthau, to Barbra Streisand

137

Boiled down to essentials, she is a plain mortal with large feet.

Herbert Kretzner, on screen goddess Greta Garbo

Age cannot wither her, nor custom stale her infinite sameness.

David Shipmanon, on Marlene Dietrich

If you weren't the best light comedian in the country, all you'd be fit for would
be the selling of cars in Great Portland Street.

Noël Coward to Rex Harrison, star of My Fair Lady

Costner has feathers in his hair and feathers in his head.

Pauline Kael, on Kevin Costner in Dances with Wolves

The trouble with Tony Curtis is that he's interested only in tight pants and wide
billing.

Billy Wilder, movie director, who directed the actor in Some Like it Hot

She does her own schtick... but she doesn't do anything she hasn't already done.
She's playing herself—and it's awfully soon for that.

Pauline Kael, film critic, on Barbra Streisand's performance in
What's Up, Doc?

A testicle with legs.

Pauline Kael, film critic, on diminutive British actor Bob Hoskins

Kristofferson looked like the Werewolf of London stoned on cocaine and sounded like a dying buffalo.

Rex Reed, on Kris Kristofferson in A Star is Born

[Miss Dennis] has made an acting style out of postnasal drip.

Pauline Kael, film critic, on the actress Sandy Dennis

A passionate amoeba.

David Susskind, talk-show host, about the actor Tony Curtis

Necking with Marilyn Monroe is like kissing Hitler.

Tony Curtis, who starred with Marilyn in the movie Some Like it Hot

She speaks five languages and can't act in any of them.

John Gielgud, about Ingrid Bergman (reprising Dorothy Parker's famous jibe)

Scumbag.

Ed Asner, on Charlton Heston

Charlton Heston throws all his punches in the first ten minutes (three grimaces and two intonations) so that he has nothing left long before he stumbles to the end, four hours later, and has to react to the crucifixion. (He does make it clear, I must admit, that he disapproves of it.)

Dwight MacDonald, on Charlton Heston's performance in the epic movie Ben Hur

His features resembled a fossilized wash rag.

Alan Brien, about Steve McQueen

Elizabeth Taylor is the first Cleopatra to sail down the Nile to Las Vegas.

Review of the 1963 movie Cleopatra

Save for direction, story, dialog, acting, and being a period picture, this is a
good one.

The US magazine Variety, *on the British film* The American Prisoner

That's what you think.

James Agee, on the film You Were Meant for Me

His ears make him look like a taxicab with both doors open.

Howard Hughes, onetime director, on Clark Gable

Clark Gable has the best ears of our lives.

Milton Berle

The entire evening gave me a headache for which suicide seemed the only
possible relief.

Rex Reed, critic, on The Rocky Horror Picture Show

He got a reputation as a great actor just by thinking hard about the next line.

King Vidor, movie director, about Gary Cooper

Most of the time he sounds like he has a mouth full of wet toilet paper.

Rex Reed, critic, on Marlon Brando

And to Hell it can go!

Ed Naha, on the 1959 schlock-horror movie From Hell It Came

This film needs something. Possibly burial.

David Larner, on the movie Panama Hattie

That red, thin, sharp snout—it reminds you of an anteater.

Truman Capote, on Meryl Streep

Joan Collins is to acting what her sister Jackie is to literature.

The London Daily Express *newspaper on the famous Collins duo*

If white bread could sing, it would sound like Olivia Newton-John.

Anon. critic, on the star of the hit movie Grease

A picture to throw up by.

Tom Skerrit, actor, on The Devil's Rain, *a movie starring John Travolta*

Any of my indiscretions were with people, not actresses.

Darryl F. Zanuck, movie mogul

Miss Minnelli has only two things going for her—a father and a mother who got
her there in the first place, and tasteless reviewers and audiences who keep
her there.

John Simon, critic, on Liza Minnelli

That turnipy nose overhanging a forward-gaping mouth and hastily retreating
chin, that bulbous cranium with eyes as big (and as inexpressive) as saucers...

John Simon, critic, on Liza Minnelli

She is not even an actress, only a trollop.

Gloria Swanson, on Lana Turner

The worst and most homeliest thing to hit the screens since Liza Minnelli.

John Simon, about Shelley Duvall

Martin's acting is so inept that even his impersonation of a lush seems
unconvincing.

Harry Medved, on Dean Martin

Actress: "I dread the thought of 45."
Rosalind Russell, actress: "Why, what happened to you then, dear?"

I cannot say that Mailer was drunk the whole time he was on camera. I can only
hope that he was drunk.

Stanley Kauffmann, on Mailer's performance in Wild 90,
reported in The New Republic

A swaggering, tough little slut.

Louise Brooks, on child star Shirley Temple

She was fine when she was six or seven. But did you notice how she couldn't
act when she was fourteen?

Tatum O'Neal, on Shirley Temple

Manifestly subliterate.

John Simon, critic, on rival critic Rex Reed

Who? I never criticize my elders.

Sophia Loren, on fellow Italian actress Gina Lollobrigida

Working with her was like being bombed by watermelons.

Alan Ladd, on Sophia Loren

Madonna was guilty as hell. Her crime is that she just can't act, not with one
stitch—or stitchless.

USA Today, on Madonna's performance in Body of Evidence

He is to acting what Liberace was to pumping iron.

Rex Reed, critic, about Sylvester Stallone

She's the kind of girl who climbed the ladder of success, wrong by wrong.

Mae West, on fellow film star, Jean Harlow

Silicon from the knees up.

George Masters, critic, on Raquel Welsh

Whatever happened to John Travolta? I heard he joined some cult and got fat.
Or he married and had a child. Which amounts to the same thing.

Gerard Depardieu, on John Travolta

[She was] dressed in a *peignoir* of beige lace... with a blonde wig above false
eyelashes—a kind of Mt. Rushmore of the cosmetician's art.

Dwight Whitney, on Mae West

I didn't know you ever had, darling.

*John Barrymore, responding to the relief expressed by Katharine
Hepburn at completing a film (A Bill of Divorcement) with him,
and not having to act with him any more*

Her voice is a cross between Donald Duck and a Stradivarius.

Anon., on Katharine Hepburn

A plumber's idea of Cleopatra.

W. C. Fields, on Mae West

If people don't sit at Chaplin's feet, he goes out and stands where they are
sitting.

Herman J. Mankiewicz, on star of the silent era Charlie Chaplin

When Chaplin found a voice to say what was on his mind, he was like a child of
eight writing lyrics for Beethoven's Ninth.

Billy Wilder, on Charlie Chaplin

Olivier brandished his technique like a kind of stylistic alibi. In catching the eye,
he frequently disengaged the brain.

Russell Davies, on Laurence Olivier

The last time I saw him he was walking down Lover's Lane holding his
own hand.

Fred Allen

He never bore a grudge against anyone he wronged.

Simone Signoret

Several tons of dynamite are set off in this John Wayne picture—none of it under
the right people.

James Agee, on yet another Wayne western

He delivered his lines with the emotional fervor of a conductor announcing
local stops.

The New Yorker *on Paul Newman's performance in* The Silver Chalice

His voice is something between bland and grandiose: blandiose perhaps.

Kenneth Tynan, on Sir Ralph Richardson

145

I am able to look at my wife again and not want to hit her because she is
a woman.

> *Billy Wilder, confiding to reporters at the end of filming*
> Some Like It Hot *(the admission expressed relief at not having to*
> *deal with Marilyn Monroe–the movie's star--on a daily basis)*

It was like having a demented, highly intelligent parrot in the house.

> *Quentin Tarantino's mother, on the director as a young boy*

Dietrich? That contraption! She was one of the beautiful-but-dumb girls, like me,
but she belonged to the category of those who thought they were smart and
fooled other people into believing it.

> *Louise Brooks, on Marlene Dietrich*

...as corny as a chiropodists' convention.

> *From a review of the movie* Strictly Ballroom

I watched *Titanic* when I got back home from the hospital, and cried. I knew
then that my IQ had been damaged.

> *Stephen King*

Show me a great actor and I'll show you a lousy husband; show me a great
actress, and you've seen the devil.

> *W. C. Fields*

The only... talent that Miss Day possesses is that of being absolutely sanitary:
her personality untouched by human emotions, her brow unclouded by
human thought, her form unsmudged by the slightest evidence of femininity.

John Simon, on Doris Day

Seagulls, as the film stresses, subsist on garbage, and, I guess, you are what
you eat.

John Simon, on the film Jonathan Livingston Seagull

Her figure resembles the giant economy-sized tube of toothpaste in girls'
bathrooms: squeezed intemperately at all points, it acquires a shape that
defies definition by the most resourceful solid geometrician.

John Simon, on Judy Garland

He's the type of man who will end up dying in his own arms.

' Mamie Van Doren, on Warren Beatty

Everyone is going on about how great Julia was in *Erin Brockovich*, but what
did she actually do? Wear push-up bras. It wasn't great acting.

Eric Roberts, on his sister, Julia Roberts

A cross between an aardvark and an albino rat surmounted by a platinum-
coated horse bun. Though she has good eyes and a nice complexion, the rest
of her is a veritable anthology of disaster areas.

John Simon, on the acting talents–or otherwise–of Barbra Streisand

Dorothy Parker

If all the young ladies who attended the Yale promenade dance were laid end to end, no one would be the least surprised.

Of female Ivy League students

Clare Boothe Luce, to Dorothy Parker, as they met in a doorway: "Age before beauty!"

Parker's response as she swept through it ahead of her: "Pearls before swine!"

You can lead a whore-to-culture but you can't make her think.

On being challenged to use the word "horticulture" in a sentence

Outspoken by whom?

To a gushing female who had approached, launching in with "You'll think I'm terribly outspoken…"

That's queer. Your mother could.

To a pompous individual who had declared, "I can't bear fools"

That woman speaks eighteen languages and can't say "No" in any of them.

On a guest at one of her parties

Look at him, a rhinestone in the rough.

On an unknown individual

At least something in the play is moving.

On an actress who should have been wearing a stronger corset

He hasn't got enough sense to bore a**holes in wooden hobbyhorses.

On an unknown Hollywood producer

Promises, promises.

On being told by her physician that she would be dead within a month if she didn't stop drinking

How can they tell?

On hearing of the death of President Coolidge

If you don't mind my saying so, I think you're full of skit.

To an American actor recently returned from London, and adopting the English way of pronouncing "skedule"

Acquaintance, chatting merrily away: "Anyway, she's very nice to her inferiors."
Parker: "Where does she find them?"

Related of an unknown individual

She has two expressions: joy and indigestion.

On the film actress Marion Davies

To me, Edith looks like something that would eat its young.

On the actress Dame Edith Evans

I require only three things of a man. He must be handsome, ruthless, and stupid.

On men in general

Scratch an actor and you'll find an actress.

On actors in general

I think that they crawl back into the woodwork.

Whispered reply to Alexander Woollcott, at a country-house weekend
where Woollcott had wondered aloud about the usual habitat of the
other guests. Recounted by Woollcott in While Rome Burns

Good work, Mary. We all knew you had it in you.

In a congratulatory wire to an acquaintance who had given birth
(the woman in question had bored the neighborhood with her
"delicate'" condition)

The affair between Margot Asquith and Margot Asquith will live as one of the
prettiest love stories in all literature.

On a four-volume (!) autobiography of Margot Asquith,
English society hostess and wife of the Prime Minister

Theater

An enchanting toad of a man.

> Helen Hayes, on critic and author Robert Benchley

Me Bobby. Bobby bad boy. Me go.

> Robert Benchley, irritated by the excessive use of Pidgin English
> in a play called The Squall, thus exiting its 1926 premiere (the
> final straw had been when an actress fell to her knees, pleading,
> "Me Nubi. Nubi good girl. Me stay.")

An ego like a raging tooth.

> W. B. Yeats, on the actress Mrs. Patrick Campbell

Ladies, just a little more virginity, if you don't mind.

> Herbert Beerbohm Tree, to a group of female extras rehearsing
> for a New York production of Henry VIII, in which Tree
> was playing Wolsey

He writes his plays for the ages—the ages between five and twelve.

George Jean Nathan, on George Bernard Shaw

It should have been called *A Month in the Wrong Country.*

Noël Coward, on an American adaptation of Anton Checkhov's
The Cherry Orchard *transplanted to the Deep South of the United States*

The first rule is not to write like Henry Arthur Jones. The second and third rules
are the same.

Oscar Wilde, on a then prolific and popular—but
hollow—playwright

My dear Sir,

I have read your play.

Oh, my dear Sir.

Yours faithfully...

Signing-off from Henry Beerbohm Tree, to an aspiring playwright

Mrs. Patrick Campbell, to the producer of George Bernard Shaw's play,
Pygmalion, in which she was starring on Broadway: "Always remember, Mr.
Froham, that I am an artist."
Charles Froham: "Your secret's safe with me."

Shaw isn't a dramatist. He is a journalist with a sense of the theater.

Henry Arthur Jones, regarding George Bernard Shaw

Mr. Steyne's performance was the worst to be seen in the contemporary
theater.

> *Heywood Broun, on the actor Geoffrey Steyne, who promptly*
> *sued him for libel. Broun, true to form, followed up the attack*
> *with a review of Steyne's performance in another play, as follows:*
> *"Mr. Steyne's performance was not up to his usual standard."*

I could never understand what he saw in her until I saw her at the Caprice
eating corn-on-the-cob.

> *Coral Browne, Australian actress, spiking an unknown*
> *female target*

Those people on the stage are making such a noise I can't hear a word you're
saying.

> *Henry Taylor Parker, music critic, in an attempt to hush members*
> *of the audience*

The sort of show that gives pornography a bad name.

> *Clive Barnes on the musical* Oh, Calcutta!

No.

> *Review in a London newspaper of a show called* A Good Time, *which ran at*
> *the Duchess Theatre in the early 1900s*

No!

> *Hannen Swaffer, reviewing the show* Yes and No

Religion and atheism will both survive it.

Stanley Kauffmann on the musical Jesus Christ Superstar *by*
Tim Rice and Andrew Lloyd Webber

The play performed last night is simple enough in plan and purpose, but simple
only in the sense of an open drain; of a loathsome sore unbandaged; of a dirty
act done publicly; or of a lazar-house with all its doors and windows open.

The London Daily Telegraph, *commenting on Ibsen's* Ghosts *in 1891,*
on the occasion of its first English language production

An open drain... the sort of play that requires ammonia.

Contemporary reaction to Ibsen's Ghosts—*on its Victorian premiere it was*
received with outrage and disgust

A day away from Tallulah is like a month in the country.

Howard Dietz, on Tallulah Bankhead

My dear girl, good is not the word...

Max Beerbohm, to an actress after a poor performance

The best thing about Ian McKellen's Hamlet was his curtain call.

Harold Hobson, London theater critic

Darling, I don't care what anybody says—I thought you were marvellous.

Beatrice Lillie, delivering a back-handed backstage compliment

For those who missed it the first time, this is your golden opportunity: you can miss it again.

> *Michael Billington*, The Guardian *newspaper's theater critic,*
> *of a revival of the musical* Godspell *in 1981*

Mr. Clarke played the King all evening as though under constant fear that someone else was about to play the ace.

> *Eugene Field, on Creston Clarke's performance as King Lear in*
> *Shakespeare's play of that name*

I have knocked everything but the knees of the chorus girls, and nature has anticipated me there.

> *Percy Hammond, theater critic*

Oh for an hour of Herod!

> *Anthony Hope on the first night of J. M. Barrie's classic play* Peter Pan

Chew on that, you walruses, while the rest of us get on with the libretto.

> *John Barrymore, addressing an audience wracked with coughing—and*
> *throwing it a fish into the bargain. Recorded by John Train in* Wit

Like the skins of a small mammal, just not large enough to be used as mats.

> *Max Beerbohm, on the eyebrows of the playwright Arthur Wing Pinero*

Yours, with admiration and detestation.

> *Sir Arthur Wing Pinero, signing off a letter to fellow playwright*
> *George Bernard Shaw*

Prompter steals the show in U.C.L.A. *Macbeth*.

> *Los Angeles Times* headline

Very well then: I say Never.

> *George Jean Nathan, on a play by the name of* Tonight or Never

He's too clever by three-quarters.

> *Anon., on theater director Jonathan Miller*

The cheerful clatter of Sir James Barrie's cans as he went round with the milk of human kindness.

> *Philip Guadella*

Hook and Ladder is the sort of play that gives failures a bad name.

> *Walter Kerr, critic*

The scenery was beautiful but the actors got in front of it. The play left a taste of lukewarm parsnip juice.

> *Alexander Woollcott*

He delivers every line with a monotonous tenor bark as if addressing an
audience of Eskimos who have never heard of Shakespeare.

The Guardian *newspaper on Peter O'Toole's performance as*
Macbeth at the Old Vic in London

The first man to have cut a swathe through the theater and left it strewn with
virgins.

Frank Harris, on George Bernard Shaw

An affair between a mad rocking-horse and a rawhide suitcase.

Noël Coward, on Jeanette MacDonald and Nelson Eddy in Bitter Sweet

There is absolutely nothing wrong with Oscar Levant that a miracle can't fix.

Alexander Woollcott

I didn't pay three pounds fifty just to see half a dozen acorns and a chipolata.

Noël Coward, on a (male) nude scene in the play The Changing Room

I'm a very old lady. I may die during one of your pauses.

Dame Edith Evans, actress, upbraiding a young actress with a
particular fondness for lengthy pauses

A sort of Cockney Ivy Compton-Burnett.

Noël Coward, on the British playwright Harold Pinter

It seems to me that giving Clive Barnes his CBE for services to the theater is like giving Goering the DFC for services to the RAF.

Alan Bennett, on a British-born drama critic on Broadway

Vera, vera, bad.

The British satirical magazine Punch, *on Oscar Wilde's play* Vera or The Nihilists—*which ran for a short time, then flopped*

If you ask me what *Uncle Vanya* is about, I would say about as much as I can take.

Robert Garland, on a production of Anton Chekhov's play, from Journal American

Fallen archness.

Franklin Pierce Adams, on the actress Helen Hayes's performance as Cleopatra in a 1925 production of George Bernard Shaw's play Caesar and Cleopatra

I do not want actors and actresses to understand my plays. That is not necessary. If they will only pronounce the correct sounds I can guarantee the results.

George Bernard Shaw

I've just spent an hour talking to Tallulah for a few minutes.

Fred Keating, about the actress Tallulah Bankhead

THE BIGGEST ASP DISASTER IN THE WORLD.

> *Newspaper headline on the Charlton Heston remake of*
> Antony and Cleopatra

Shakespeare is so tiring. You never get a chance to sit down unless you're
a king.

> *Josephine Hull*

Cable from George Bernard Shaw on the opening of a revival of his play
Candida: "Excellent. Greatest."
Cabled reply from the actress Cornelia Otis Skinner: "Undeserving of
such praise."
Shaw: "I meant the play."
Skinner: "So did I."

A theatrical whore of the first quality.

> *Peter Hall, British theater director, on Bertolt Brecht*

Why don't you just roll on your Rs?

> *Jerome Kern, to an irritating actress in* Show Boat, *who rolled her
> Rs melodramatically and was complaining about how she was
> going to get from one side of the stage to the other*

Critics? I love every bone in their heads.

> *Eugene O'Neill, playwright*

Watching your performance from the rear of the house. Wish you were here.

> *George S. Kaufman, in a note to William Gaxton, the lead actor in G.S.K.'s*
> *play* Of Thee I Sing; *Gaxton, becoming bored with the role after a long run,*
> *had turned in an especially lacklustre performance*

It was a bad play saved by a bad performance.

> *George S. Kaufman, on the actress Gertrude Lawrence in a*
> *play called* Skylark

I didn't like the play but then I saw it under adverse conditions—the curtain
   was up.

> *Groucho Marx*

You know I can't stand Shakespeare's plays, but yours are even worse.

> *Leo Tolstoy, to Anton Chekhov, after seeing* Uncle Vanya

Perfectly Scandalous was one of those plays in which all the actors,
   unfortunately, enunciated very clearly.

> *Robert Benchley*

Eleven A.M. rehearsal tomorrow morning to remove all improvements to the
   play inserted since the last rehearsal.

> *George S. Kaufman, in a callboard note left for the cast of a play*
> *of his which was still in rehearsal*

...a confidence trick perpetrated on the twentieth century by a theater-hating
God.

> *Sheridan Morley, British critic, on Irish playwright Samuel*
> *Beckett in the satirical magazine* Punch

She was so dramatic she stabbed the potatoes at dinner.

> *Sydney Smith, on Mrs. Sarah Siddons, 18th-century dramatic*
> *actress*

Actor: "Has anybody got a nickel? I have to phone a friend."
George S. Kaufman: "Here's a dime–phone all of them."

Tallulah Bankhead barged down the Nile last night as Cleopatra—and sank.

> *John Mason Brown, on Tallulah's performance in* Antony and Cleopatra

Ah, forgotten but not gone.

> *George S. Kaufman, on coming across S. N. Behrman, whose farewell party*
> *in Hollywood G. S. K. had attended only a few days before*

Tiresome hussy.

> *Henry Arthur Jones, regarding Henrik Ibsens's heroine Nora, in*
> The Doll's House

There is less in this than meets the eye.

> *Comment by Tallulah Bankhead to Alexander Woollcott, while*
> *watching a revival of Maeterlinck's* Aglavine and Selysette

Superabundance of foulness... wholly immoral and degenerate... you cannot
have a clean pig sty.

> *Contemporary newspaper editorial letting rip on George Bernard Shaw's*
> play *Mrs. Warren's Profession*

Dramatized stench.

> *Contemporary review of George Bernard Shaw's* Mrs Warren's Profession

An Irish smut-dealer.

> *Anthony Comstock, Secretary for the Society for the Suppression of Vice,*
> *on George Bernard Shaw in 1905*

The program indicates that the play was undirected. The production bears this
out.

> *Walter Kerr, on the play* Abraham Cochrane

Constance Cummings and Jack Mulhall play the leading parts in *Lover Come
Back*. I am afraid it's too late now.

> *Capsule criticism courtesy of* The Los Angeles Examiner

Elizabeth Taylor, sounding something like Minnie Mouse and weighted down to
her ankles in comedic intent, keeps crashing against the trees while Richard
Burton...slogs up and down oddly majestic molehills.

> *Kevin Kelly, on a Taylor–Burton performance of*
> *Noël Coward's play* Private Lives

When Mr. Wilbur calls his play *Halfway to Hell*, he underestimates the distance.

Brooks Atkinson

Number Seven opened last night. It was misnamed by five.

Alexander Woollcott

An American musical so bad that at times I longed for the boy-meets-tractor
theme of Soviet drama.

Bernard Levin, English critic, on the musical The Flower Drum Song *in the*
London Daily Express *newspaper*

...all ends happily, especially the audience, who can finally go home—I mean
those few who, for whatever reason, did not do so before.

John Simon, on the play Three Men on a Horse

Diana Rigg is built like a brick mausoleum with insufficient flying buttresses.

John Simon, on the English actress's nude appearance in the play
Abélard and Héloïse

If a fetchingly cleft chin can be called a performance, Schell can be said to act.

John Simon, on Maximilian Schell

He has delusions of adequacy.

Walter Kerr, on an unnamed actor

During the first number you hoped it would be good. After that you just hoped it would be over.

Walter Kerr, on the musical Buttrio Square

They shoot too many pictures and not enough actors.

Walter Winchell, columnist

Dustin Farnum, actor: "I've never been better! In the last act yesterday, I had the audience glued to their seats."
Oliver Herford, writer: "How clever of you to think of it."

Excuse me, my leg has gone to sleep. Do you mind if I join it?

Alexander Woollcott, critic, to a tedious young actor

Frank Rich and John Simon are the syphilis and gonorrhea of the theater.

David Mamet, playwright

Starlight Express is the perfect gift for the kid who has everything except parents.

Frank Rich, on the Broadway flop Starlight Express *in the* New York Times

Jones sounded like a one-stringed double bass with a faintly Calypso accent, and rolled about like a huge barrel set in motion by a homunculus within.

John Simon, critic, on James Earl Jones, in Shakespeare's Coriolanus

Talking so ceaselessly that you had to make a reservation five minutes ahead to
get a word in.

Earl Wilson, columnist, about Tallulah Bankhead

Earl Wilson, columnist, to Tallulah Bankhead: "Have you ever been mistaken for
a man?"

Tallulah Bankhead's reply: "No, darling. Have you?"

Two things should be cut: the second act and the child's throat.

Noël Coward

If they'd stuffed the child's head up the horse's arse, they would have solved
two problems at once.

Noël Coward, on a musical version of Gone with the Wind, *starring the
irritatingly cute Bonnie Langford and a horse that had just expressed
its own opinion of the piece on stage...*

He looks like an extra in a crowd scene by Hieronymous Bosch.

Kenneth Tynan, critic, on Don Rickles, comedian

The play opened at 8.40 sharp and closed at 10.40 dull.

Heywood Broun on a Broadway "comedy"

I really enjoy only his stage directions... He uses the English language like a
truncheon.

Max Beerbohm, on George Bernard Shaw

The gods bestowed on Max the gift of perpetual old age.

Oscar Wilde, on Max Beerbohm

Guido Nadzo was nadzo guido.

George S. Kaufman (attrib.) on an aspiring young Italian actor with the unfortunate name of Guido Nadzo; the comment has also been attributed to the critic Brooks Atkinson

Press agent to George S. Kaufman: "How do I get our leading lady's name in your newspaper."

G. S. K.'s reply: "Shoot her."

In the matter of soliloquies we cannot accept Hamlet as an unbiased authority. We merely find in him the possible origin of the belief that talking to oneself is a bad sign.

Max Beerbohm

His performance was not without its synthetic appeal. It was the work of an attractive, earnest, and intelligent comedian.

J. Ranken Towse on John Barrymore's performance as Hamlet in Shakespeare's tragedy of that name

Its hero is caused, by a novel device, to fall asleep and dream; and thus he is given yesterday. Me, I should have given him twenty years to life.

Dorothy Parker on Give Me Yesterday *by A. A. Milne, in* The New Yorker

In fact, now that you've got me right down to it, the only thing I didn't like about
The Barretts of Wimpole Street was the play.

> *Dorothy Parker, rounding off an extremely long review, in which she let the*
> *play simply hang itself by its own rope, in* The New Yorker

The House Beautiful is the play lousy.

> *Dorothy Parker in her one-sentence review of a play*
> *by Channing Pollock called* The House Beautiful

I'm not very good at it myself, but the first rule about spelling is that there is
only one "z" in "is."

> *George S. Kaufman, to an author whose manuscript was littered*
> *with spelling mistakes*

Go to the Martin Beck Theater and watch Katherine Hepburn run the whole
gamut of emotions from A to B.

> *Dorothy Parker on Katharine Hepburn's performance in*
> The Lake on Broadway

Farley Granger played Mr. Darcy with all the flexibility of a telegraph pole.

> *Brooks Atkinson, reviewing a musical version of* Pride and Prejudice *by*
> *Bo Goldman on Broadway in the 1950s*

I understand your new play is full of single entendre.

> *Remark by George S. Kaufman (attrib.) to Howard Dietz,*
> *author of* Between the Devil

Producer who had omitted to pay royalties due to George S. Kaufman, offering
up the excuse: "After all, it's only a small, insignificant theater."

G. S. K.'s reply: "Then you'll go to a small, insignificant jail."

So-and-so played Hamlet last night at the Tabor Grand. He played till one
o'clock.

> *Eugene Field's complete and unexpurgated review of a*
> *particularly uninspiring performance of* Hamlet

I have been looking around for an appropriate wooden gift and am pleased
hereby to present you with Elsi Ferguson's performance in her new play.

> *Alexander Woollcott in a telegram to George and Bea Kaufman on the*
> *occasion of their fifth wedding anniversary; recorded in* George S. Kaufman
> and the Algonquin Round Table *by Scott Meredith*

There was laughter at the back of the theater, leading to the belief that
someone was telling jokes back there.

> *George S. Kaufman on a "comedy" showing on Broadway*

What a glorious garden of wonders the lights of Broadway would be to anyone
lucky enough to be unable to read.

> *G. K. Chesterton*

He looked like something that had gotten loose from Macy's Thanksgiving Day
Parade.

> *Harpo Marx, on Alexander Woollcott*

A great actress, from the waist down.

>> *Dame Margaret Kendal, on the dramatic actress Sarah Bernhardt*

Massey won't be satisfied until someone assassinates him.

>> *George S. Kaufman, referring to the pompous airs adopted by the*
>> *actor Raymond Massey, fresh from his success in the part of*
>> *Abraham Lincoln in a play on Broadway*

Oscar Wilde, to Sarah Bernhardt: "Do you mind if I smoke?"
Sarah Bernhardt's reply: "I don't care if you burn."

Method acting? There are quite a few methods. Mine involves a lot of talent, a glass, and some cracked ice.

>> *John Barrymore*

I could eat alphabet soup and s**t better lyrics.

>> *Johnny Mercer, American lyricist, on the first night of an*
>> *unnamed British musical*

She was a large woman who seemed not so much dressed as upholstered.

>> *J. M. Barrie, demolishing an unknown target*

Another week's rehearsal with WSG and I should have gone raving mad. I had already ordered some straw for my hair.

>> *Sir Arthur Sullivan on Sir William Schwenck Gilbert*

Your skin has been acting at any rate.

> *Sir William Schwenck Gilbert, to a perspiring Sir Herbert Beerbohm Tree*
> *after a terrible first-night performance*

No madam, he's decomposing.

> *Sir William Schwenck Gilbert, to a woman at a party who had*
> *asked him whether J. S. Bach was still composing*

...irresponsible braggart; blaring self-trumpeter; idol of opaque intellectuals and
thwarted females; calculus of contrariwise; flibbertigibbet pope of chaos...

> *Henry Arthur Jones, on fellow playwright George Bernard Shaw*

Shaw's plays are the price we pay for Shaw's prefaces.

> *James Agate, in his diary entry for March 10, 1933*

Would that he had blotted a thousand.

> *Ben Jonson, Shakespeare's supposed rival, in the wake of the*
> *surprise discovery that the bard's manuscripts contained very*
> *few blotted-out lines*

Reading him is like wading through glue.

> *Tennyson, on Ben Jonson*

No one can have a higher opinion of him than I have–and I think he is a dirty
little beast.

> *Sir William Schwenck Gilbert–on a friend!*

When you were quite a little boy somebody ought to have said "hush" just once.

Mrs. Patrick Campbell, actress, to George Bernard Shaw

To many, no doubt, he will seem blatant and bumptious, but we prefer to regard him as being simply British.

The Pall Mall Gazette *of London, on Irish-born Oscar Wilde*

The play was a great success, but the audience was a disaster.

Oscar Wilde

The central problem in *Hamlet* is whether the critics are mad or only pretending to be mad.

Oscar Wilde

God be pleased to make the breath stink and the teeth rot out of them all therefore!

Charles Lamb, cursing the audience that had booed his play

Watching Tallulah on stage is like watching somebody skating on thin ice. Everyone wants to be there when it breaks.

Mrs. Patrick Campbell, English actress, on the American actress Tallulah Bankhead

... so helpless, so crude, so bad, so clumsy, feeble, and vulgar.

Henry James on Oscar Wilde's new play, An Ideal Husband

Noël Coward

Too much wood; too little cock.

To a restaurant waiter, who had asked how he was enjoying the woodcock

He must have been an incredibly good shot.

On being told that someone had blown his brains out

Dear Desk...

On replying to a letter which had read "From the Desk of..."

He's a little man, that's his trouble. Never trust a man with short legs—brains too near their bottoms.

On an unknown individual

Lady Diana Cooper: "I saw your play, Noël, but I didn't laugh once I'm afraid."
Coward: "Didn't you darling? I saw yours and simply roared."

The play in question was a religious piece called The Miracle, *in which Diana was cast as a motionless statue*

I see her as one great stampede of lips directed at the nearest derriere.

On a sycophantic female

She had much in common with Hitler, only no moustache.

On an unfortunate female

The food was so abominable that I used to cross myself before I took a
mouthful. I used to say, "Ian, it tastes like armpits."

On the inedible fare on offer at Ian Fleming's home

I don't believe in astrology. The only stars I can blame for my failures are those
that walk about the stage.

She's one of those high-hatting dames. She'd high-hat her own father if she
knew who he was.

On a female with superior airs

Frankly, my dear, I should bury it and put a lily on it.

On reading a "friend's" first attempt at writing

Journalist: "Mr. Coward, haven't you anything to say to *The Star*?"
Noël Coward: "Twinkle!"

I have stopped swearing. Now I just say "Zsa Zsa Gabor."

On the Hollywood sex symbol

Showbiz

I think that's what they call professional courtesy.

Herman Manckiewicz, Hollywood screen writer, to an agent who had boasted of swimming (unharmed) in shark-infested waters

You're like a pay toilet, aren't you? You don't give a s**t for nothing.

Howard Hughes, to Robert Mitchum

Who picks your clothes—Stevie Wonder?

Don Rickles, to David Letterman

She's got a great-looking husband, a little boy, and all the money in the world. She hasn't got the looks, but you can't have everything.

Jordan, model, on Victoria Beckham, a.k.a Posh Spice

The fastest way to a man's heart is through his chest.

Roseanne Barr

It is true that I never should have married, but I didn't want to live without a
man. Brought up to respect the conventions, love had to end in marriage. I'm
afraid it did.

Bette Davis

She has proved beyond doubt that diamonds are the hardest things in the
world—to get back.

An ex-boyfriend on Zsa Zsa Gabor

I never hated a man enough to give his diamonds back.

Zsa Zsa Gabor

He taught me housekeeping; when I divorce I keep the house.

Zsa Zsa Gabor

We were both in love with him. I fell out of love with him, but he didn't.

Zsa Zsa Gabor

When you go to the mind reader, do you get half price?

David Letterman

She looks like she combs her hair with an eggbeater.

Louella Parsons, on Joan Collins

She's the original good time that was had by all.

Bette Davis, on an overly available starlet of her day

Of course they have, or I wouldn't be sitting here talking to someone like you.

Barbara Cartland, when asked by BBC interviewer Sandra Harris
whether she thought class barriers had broken down in England

Nice of you to come, but your head's too small for the camera, you are too thin, and . . . I don't know what it is exactly about the neck . . . but it's not right.

Studio executive Earl St. John to English actor Dirk Bogarde,
auditioning at Rank Organization

Yes, odd isn't it? She looked as though butter wouldn't melt in her mouth—or anywhere else.

Elsa Lanchester, on Maureen O'Hara

Another dirty shirt-tail actor from New York.

Hedda Hopper, gossip columnist, on the actor James Dean

The only reason he had a child is so that he can meet babysitters.

David Letterman, about Warren Beatty

He couldn't ad-lib a fart after a baked-bean dinner.

Johnny Carson, about Chevy Chase

He acts like he's got a Mixmaster up his ass and doesn't want anyone to know it.

Marlon Brando, on Montgomery Clift

Steve Martin has basically one joke and he's it.

Dave Felton

Now there sits a man with an open mind. You can feel the draft from here.

Groucho Marx, about his brother Chico Marx

She's so pure, Moses couldn't even part her knees.

Joan Rivers, about Marie Osmond

He has turned almost alarmingly blond—he's gone past platinum, he must be
plutonium; his hair is co-ordinated with his teeth.

Pauline Kael, on Robert Redford

Poor little man, they made him out of lemon Jell-O and there he is. He's honest
and hardworking, but he's not great.

Adela Rogers St. John, on Robert Redford

Well at least he has finally found his true love—what a pity he can't marry
himself.

Frank Sinatra, on Robert Redford

His favorite exercise is climbing tall people.

Phyllis Diller, on Mickey Rooney

Arnold Schwarzenegger looks like a condom full of walnuts.

Clive James, on the Californian Governor Formerly Known as Arnie...

He has the vocal modulation of a railway station announcer, the expressive
power of a fence post, and the charisma of a week-old head of lettuce.

Fintan O'Toole, film critic, about Quentin Tarantino

She has discovered the secret of perpetual middle age.

Oscar Levant, on Zsa Zsa Gabor

The only person who ever left the Iron Curtain wearing it.

Oscar Levant, on Zsa Zsa Gabor

You can calculate Zsa Zsa Gabor's age by the rings on her fingers.

Bob Hope

Zsa Zsa Gabor has been married so many times she has rice marks on her face.

Henny Youngman

She not only kept her lovely figure, she's added so much to it.

Bob Fosse

Her body has gone to her head.

Barbara Stanwyck, on Marilyn Monroe

She has breasts of granite and a mind like a Gruyere cheese.

Billy Wilder, on Marilyn Monroe

She's a vacuum with nipples.

Otto Preminger, on Marilyn Monroe

Elizabeth Taylor looks like two small boys fighting underneath a thick blanket.

Mr. Blackwell

Elizabeth Taylor's so fat she puts mayonnaise on aspirin.

Joan Rivers

Is she fat? She wore yellow and ten schoolchildren got aboard. Her favorite food
is seconds. She's so fat she's my two best friends. She wears stretch kaftans.
She's got more chins than the Chinese telephone directory.

Joan Rivers, on Elizabeth Taylor

Elizabeth Taylor is wearing Orson Welles-designed jeans.

Joan Rivers

Every minute this broad spends outside of bed is a waste of time.

Michael Todd, about Elizabeth Taylor

She has an insipid double chin, her legs are too short, and she has a slight
potbelly.

Richard Burton, on Elizabeth Taylor

Her hair lounges on her shoulders like an anaesthetised cocker spaniel.

Henry Allen, about Lauren Bacall

A buxom milkmaid reminiscent of a cow wearing a girdle, and both have the same amount of acting talent.

Mr. Blackwell, on Brigitte Bardot

She was so ugly she could make a mule back away from an oat bin.

Will Rogers

Joan always cries a lot. Her tear ducts must be close to her bladder.

Bette Davis, on Joan Crawford

Those eyebrows wound up looking like African caterpillars!

Bette Davis, on Joan Crawford

A kind of cross between Julia Roberts and Jack Nicholson.

Jeremy Novick, on Lolita Davidovich

She turned down the role of Helen Keller because she couldn't remember the lines.

Joan Rivers, about Bo Derek

Hah! I always knew Frank would end up in bed with a boy!

Ava Gardner, on Mia Farrow's marriage to Frank Sinatra

Dramatic art in her opinion is knowing how to fill a sweater.

Bette Davis, about Jayne Mansfield

Miss United Dairies herself.

David Niven, about Jayne Mansfield

The Russians love Brooke Shields because her eyebrows remind them of Leonid
Brezhnev.

Robin Williams

It's a new low for actresses when you have to wonder what's between her ears
instead of her legs.

Katharine Hepburn, about Sharon Stone

Whatever it was that this actress never had, she still hasn't got it.

Bosley Crowther, on Loretta Young

Roseanne Barr is a bowling ball looking for an alley.

Mr. Blackwell

The closest thing to Roseanne Barr's singing the national anthem was my cat
being neutered.

Johnny Carson

She is as much fun as barbed wire.

Tom Hutchinson, on Sandra Bernhard

I treasure every moment that I do not see her.

Oscar Levant, on Phyllis Diller

When it comes to acting, Joan Rivers has the range of a wart.

Stewart Klein

No. The "t" is silent. As in "Harlow."

Margot Asquith, English writer and wife of the Prime Minister
Herbert Asquith, to actress Jean Harlow, who had asked her
whether the "t" in "Margot" was pronounced

I didn't know her well, but after watching her in action I didn't want to know
her well.

Joan Crawford, on Judy Garland

She ought to be arrested for loitering in front of an orchestra.

Bette Midler, on Helen Reddy

Oh my God, look at you. Anyone else hurt in the accident?

Don Rickles, to Ernest Borgnine

The same person you f****d to get in.

Stephen Sondheim, to an actor who had complained,
*"Who do I have to f*** to get out of this show?"*

Saw off her legs and count the rings.

Thus interjected Carol Matthau, wife of Walter Matthau,
on discovering her husband with an older woman
and hearing him ask her how old she was

As you watch the Gary Condit interview, three words come to mind: stiff, unbending, and impenetrable... and that's just his hair.

David Letterman

He's an old bore. Even the grave yawns for him.

Herbert Beerbohm Tree, on Israel Zangwill

I knew Doris Day before she was a virgin.

Groucho Marx (Oscar Levant said the same thing)

He's a male chauvinistic piglet.

Betty Friedan, feminist author, on Groucho Marx

Ah, Victor, still struggling to keep your head below water?

Emlyn Williams, to the actor Victor Spinetti

Such a pretty face—and now there's another face around it.

Lillian Braithwaite, on ageing French actress Yvonne Arnaud

I never go to movies where the hero's bust is bigger than the heroine's.

Groucho Marx, replying to an invitation to a screening of Samson and Delilah, *in which Victor Mature was starring opposite Hedy Lamarr*

He's the only man who could eat an apple through a tennis racquet.

David Niven, British actor, on toothy Darryl Zanuck

The trouble, Mr Goldwyn, is that you are only interested in art, and I am only
interested in money.

Telegraph from George Bernard Shaw to Sam Goldwyn

He rose without trace.

Kitty Muggeridge, on David Frost

Well, it only proves what they always say—give the public what they want to
see and they'll come out for it.

Red Skelton, movie actor, commenting on the large crowd at
movie mogul Harry Cohn's funeral in 1958 (also attributed to
Sam Goldwyn about Louis B. Mayer's funeral, in the same year)

I've been doing the Fonda workout: the Peter Fonda workout. That's where I
wake up, take a hit of acid, smoke a joint, and run to my sister's house and ask
her for money.

Kevin Meaney

Working for Warner Brothers is like f*****g a porcupine–it's one hundred pricks
against one.

Wilson Mizner

Oh, what a pretty dress—and so cheap!

Zsa Zsa Gabor, "complimenting" another woman

A face to launch a thousand dredgers.

Jack de Manio, on actress Glenda Jackson

Joan Rivers: "Besides your husband, who's the best man you've ever been in
  bed with?"

Joan Collins: "Your husband."

Joan Rivers: "Funny, he didn't say the same about you."

She is the kind of girl who will not go anywhere without her mother. And her
  mother will go anywhere.

John Barrymore, on his ex-wife Elaine

There's a broad with her future behind her.

Constance Bennett (attrib.), about Marilyn Monroe

I never forget a face—but I'll make an exception in your case.

Groucho Marx, to a fan who had been overly familiar with him

A bona fide fashion fiasco—from nose to toe she's the tacky tattooed terror.

Mr. Blackwell on Cher

Diana is a horse's ass; quite a pretty one, but still a horse's ass.

John Barrymore, on Diana Barrymore

He's so small, he's a waste of skin.

Fred Allen

Her hat is a creation that will never go out of style. It will look ridiculous year after year.

Fred Allen

I love my cigar too, but I take it out once in a while.

Groucho Marx, on the TV show You Bet Your Life, *where he was interviewing a woman who had over 20 children, weakly giving Marx as her reason, "I love my husband"*

The best time I ever had with Joan Crawford was when I pushed her down the stairs in *Whatever Happened to Baby Jane.*

Bette Davis—the feeling was entirely mutual

I wouldn't sit on her toilet.

Bette Davis, about Joan Crawford

Joan Crawford—Hollywood's first case of syphilis.

Bette Davis, about Joan Crawford

God was very good to the world. He took her from us.

Bette Davis, on the actress Miriam Hopkins

Boiled or fried?

> *W. C. Fields' response to someone who had asked him whether*
> *he liked children*

I always keep a supply of stimulant handy in case I see a snake–which I also
keep handy.

> *W. C. Fields*

I am free of all prejudice. I hate everyone equally.

> *W. C. Fields*

I thought I told you to wait in the car.

> *Tallulah Bankhead, to a man at a party who had rushed up to*
> *greet her, exclaiming "I haven't seen you for forty-one years!"'*

Bette and I are very good friends. There's nothing I wouldn't say to her face—
both of them.

> *Tallulah Bankhead, on fellow actress Bette Davis, as a way of getting her*
> *own back on the latter's impersonation of her in the movie* All About Eve

You had to stand in line to hate him.

> *Hedda Hopper, gossip columnist, on movie producer Harry Cohn*

She was good at playing abstract confusion in the same way that a midget is
good at being short.

> *Clive James, critic, on the acting talents (or otherwise) of Marilyn Monroe*

Standing downwind [Robert] Mitchum is probably the sexiest guy going today.

Joan Rivers

I approached reading his review the way some people anticipate anal warts.

Roseanne Barr, referring to Los Angeles Daily News *critic Ray Richmond's response to her husband, Tom Arnold's, performance in a show*

This town is a back-stabbing, scum-sucking, small-minded town, but thanks for the money.

Roseanne Barr, in an advertisement taken out in the Hollywood Reporter

A very old tadpole.

Lilli Palmer, actress, on gossip columnist Louella Parsons

There wasn't a wet eye in the place.

Julie Baumgold, writer, on the wedding of Donald Trump to Martha Marples

I've had them both, and I don't think much of either.

Beatrix Lehmann, watching the couple in question tie the knot at a Hollywood wedding

Pardon me, ma'am, I thought you were a guy I knew in Pittsburgh.

Groucho Marx, peering under the hat of none other than Greta Garbo, who rewarded him with an icy stare

Hands off the threads, creep.

> *Frank Sinatra, to Hubert Humphrey, Democratic presidential*
> *candidate, who had grabbed at his suit sleeve*

I would have sex with sand before I'd have sex with Roseanne.

> *Howard Stern, shock jock, on Roseanne Barr*

Douglas had always faced a situation the only way he knew how, by running
away from it.

> *Mary Pickford, on her husband Douglas Fairbanks*

A May–December romance is one thing. BC–AD is another.

> *Jim Mullen, on the relationship between Barbra Streisand and André Agassi*

Richard Gere and Cindy Crawford—he's elastic and she's plastic.

> *Sandra Bernhard, comedienne*

Richard Gere and Cindy Crawford—his body's by Nautilus and her mind's by
Mattel.

> *Sam Kinison, comedian*

The Academy of Motion Picture Arts and Sciences? What art? What science?

> *D. W. Griffith, Hollywood director*

Copulation was, I'm sure, Marilyn's uncomplicated way of saying thank you.

> *Nunnally Johnson, about Marilyn Monroe*

Never in the history of fashion has so much material been raised so high to reveal so much that needs to be covered so badly.

Sir Cecil Beaton, fashion photographer, on the fashion for miniskirts

She's not a bad person, but stupid in terms of gray matter. I mean, I like her, but I like my dog, too.

James Caan, actor, on Bette Midler

I've seen Don entertain fifty times and I've always enjoyed his joke.

Johnny Carson, talk-show host, on Don Rickles, comedian

Try interviewing her sometime. It's like talking to a window.

Bryant Gumbel, Today show anchorman, on Jerry Hall

I have a previous engagement, which I will make as soon as possible.

John Barrymore, turning down an invitation from a renowned bore

I've read some of your modern free verse and wonder who set it free.

John Barrymore

If Clark had one inch less, he'd be the "Queen of Hollywood" instead of the king.

Carole Lombard, actress, on husband Clark Gable,
dubbed "the King of Hollywood"

If you say, "Hiya Clark, how are you?" he's stuck for an answer.

Ava Gardner, actress, on Clark Gable

His mouth is a no-go area. It's like kissing the Berlin Wall

Helena Bonham Carter, on Woody Allen

A woman went to a plastic surgeon and asked him to make her like Bo Derek.
He gave her a lobotomy.

Joan Rivers

A fellow with the inventiveness of Albert Einstein, but with the attention span
of Daffy Duck.

Tom Shales, on Robin Williams

She is as wholesome as a bowl of cornflakes and at least as sexy.

Dwight McDonald, on Doris Day

She's so stupid she returns bowling balls because they've got holes in them.

Joan Rivers, on Bo Derek

Can't act. Can't sing. Slightly bald. Can dance a little.

Screen tester, on Fred Astaire

The thief of bad gags.

Walter Winchell, columnist, on Milton Berle

She got her good looks from her father. He's a plastic surgeon.

Groucho Marx

Royals

She is a lady short on looks, absolutely deprived of any dress sense, has a figure like a Jurassic monster... very greedy when it comes to loot, no tact, and wants to upstage everyone else.

Sir Nicholas Fairbairn, MP, about Sarah Ferguson, the Duchess of York

She looked like a huge ball of fur on two well-developed legs.

Nancy Mitford, English author, about Princess Margaret

Your majesty has set out to write bad verses. And he has succeeded!

Nicolas Boileau to Louis XIV, who had turned his royal hand to poetry

I am unwell. Bring me a glass of brandy.

George, Prince of Wales (later George IV), on having kissed Caroline of Brunswick, his wife-to-be, for the first time

Courtier, to the English king: "Sire, your greatest enemy is dead."
George IV (mistaking the news of Napoleon's death for that of his unfortunate
   wife): "By God, is she?"

Now at least I know where he is.

> *The much-put-upon Queen Alexandra, to Lord Esher, shortly after*
> *the death of her husband, the English King Edward VII, who was*
> *notorious throughout his reign for his womanizing*

You have sent me a Flanders mare.

> *The English King Henry VIII, on seeing his fourth wife, Anne of Cleves,*
> *for the first time. He had agreed to the marriage having seen only a*
> *rather too flattering portrait of her by Holbein*

You've no idea what it costs to keep the old man in poverty.

> *Lord Louis Mountbatten, on Mahatma Gandhi*

The most notorious whore in all the world.

> *Peter Wentworth, on Mary, Queen of Scots*

In private life he would have been called an honest blockhead.

> *Lady Wortley Montagu, on George I*

He has the heart of a cucumber fried in snow.

> *Ninon de Lenclos (1620–1705), French courtesan,*
> *on the Marquis de Sévigné, French aristocrat*

Aristocrat to Lord Frederick North: "Who is that ugly woman who just came in?"
North's reply: "Oh, that is my wife."
Aristocrat, now embarrassed: "Sir, I beg your pardon. I do not mean her. I mean
that shocking monster who is along with her."
Lord Frederick North's reply: "That is my daughter."

Most gracious Queen, we thee implore
    To go away and sin no more,
    But if that effort be too great,
    To go away, at any rate.

Anonymous epigram on Queen Caroline, unfortunate wife of George IV

The king blew his nose twice, and wiped the royal perspiration repeatedly from
    a face which is probably the largest uncivilized spot in England.

Oliver Wendell Holmes, on William IV

The bloom of her ugliness is going off.

Colonel Disbrowe, on the ageing Queen Charlotte, wife of King George III

Anne... when in good humor, was meekly stupid, and when in bad humor, was
    sulkily stupid.

Thomas Babington Macaulay, on Queen Anne

The Church's wet nurse, Goody Anne.

Horace Walpole, on Queen Anne

One of the smallest people ever set in a great place.

Walter Bagehot, on Queen Anne

My dear firstborn is the greatest ass, and the greatest liar and the greatest
canaille (dregs) and the greatest beast in the whole world and I most heartily
wish he were out of it.

Queen Caroline II, wife of George II, on her son Frederick, Prince of Wales

I wish the ground would open this minute and sink the monster into the lowest
hole in hell.

Queen Caroline, wife of George II, on her son Frederick, Prince of Wales

Here lies Fred,
Who was alive and now is dead:
Had it been his father,
I had much rather;
Had it been his brother,
Better than another;
Had it been his sister,
No one would have missed her;
Had it been the whole generation,
Better for the nation:
But since 'tis only Fred,
Who was alive and is dead –
There's no more to be said.

Horace Walpole, on Frederick, Prince of Wales

George II's famous reply to his wife, as on her deathbed she exhorted him to
marry again: "Never, I shall always take mistresses."
Queen Caroline's riposte to that: "That shouldn't hamper your marrying."

She was happy as the dey was long.

Lord Norbury, on the scandalous affair of Caroline of Brunswick—
George IV's queen—with the Muslim Dey of Algiers

One of the moral monsters of history.

Samuel Taylor Coleridge, on Charles II

Duchess of Portsmouth to Nell Gwynne, mistress of Charles II: "Why, woman,
you are fine enough to be a queen."
Nell's reply: "You are entirely right, Madam, and I am whore enough to be
a duchess."

An old, mad, blind, despised, and dying king—
Princes, the dregs of their dull race, who flow
Through public scorn—mud from a muddy spring;
Rulers who neither see, nor feel, nor know,
But leechlike to their fainting country cling,
Till they drop, blind in blood, without a blow...

Percy Bysshe Shelley, on George III et al

Through the greater part of his life, George III was a kind of consecrated obstruction.

Walter Bagehot, on George III

George the First was always reckoned
  Vile, but viler George the Second;
  And what mortal ever heard
  Any good from George the Third?
  When from Earth the Fourth descended
  (God be praised!) the Georges ended.

Walter Savage Landor, on the four Georges of England

Never was a person less mourned by his fellow men than the late King... if ever George IV had a friend, a true friend, in any social class, so we may claim that his or her name never reached our ears.

The Times *newspaper, in its obituary for George IV*

He was not a man of talent or of much refinement.

The Times *newspaper, in its obituary for William IV*

By God, you never saw such a figure in your life as he is. Then he speaks and swears so like old Falstaff, that damn me if I am not ashamed to walk into a room with him.

The Duke of Wellington, on the Prince Regent, the future king George IV

Queen Caroline: "You see how punctual I am, Duke; I am even before my time."
Wellington: "That, your majesty, is not punctuality."

The Duke of Wellington, to Queen Caroline, consort of the
unfortunate George IV

As a son, as a husband, as a father, and especially as an advisor of young men, I
deem it my duty to say that, on a review of his whole life, I can find no one
good thing to speak of, in either the conduct or the character of this king.

William Cobbett, on the English king George IV

A more contemptible, cowardly, selfish, unfeeling dog does not exist than this
King...with vices and weaknesses of the lowest and most contemptible order.

Charles Greville, diarist, on George IV

Who's your fat friend?

George "Beau" Brummell to Beau Nash, who had introduced the former to
the Prince Regent, the future King George IV

Strip your Louis Quartorze of his king gear and there is left nothing but a poor
forked radish with a head fantastically carved.

Thomas Carlyle, on the "Sun King," the French king Louis XIV

Nowadays, a parlor maid as ignorant as Queen Victoria was when she came to
the throne would be classed as mentally defective.

George Bernard Shaw, on Queen Victoria

Sir,

I am loth to interrupt the rapture of mourning in which the nation is now enjoying its favorite festival—a funeral. But in a country like ours the total suspension of common sense and sincere human feeling for a whole fortnight is an impossibility.

> *George Bernard Shaw, on the defunct Queen Victoria in a letter*
> *to the* Morning Herald—*it remained unprinted*

Very sorry can't come. Lie follows by post.

> *Baron Beresford (Charles William de la Poer), British naval officer*
> *and author of* A Life of Nelson, *replying by telegram to a last-minute*
> *dinner invitation from Edward, Prince of Wales, later Edward VIII*

I don't mind your being killed, but I object to your being taken prisoner.

> *Lord Kitchener, to the Prince of Wales, when he requested a*
> *posting to the Western Front in World War I*

A corpulent voluptuary.

> *Rudyard Kipling, on Edward VII*

... he was at his best only when the going was good.

> *Alistair Cooke, on Edward VII*

Born into the ranks of the working class, the new King's most likely fate would have been that of a street-corner loafer.

> *James Keir Hardie, Labour leader, on George V*

For 17 years he did nothing at all but kill animals and stick in stamps.

Harold Nicholson, biographer, on George V

The Billy Carter of the British monarchy.

Robert Lacey on Princess Margaret

...emotionally located in the foothills of adolescence...a frothball.

Edward Pearce, commentator, on the late Diana, Princess of Wales,
in the Guardian *newspaper*

...low-octane duds in jodhpurs.

Edward Pearce, commentator, on the British royal family
in the Guardian *newspaper*

A sort of social hand grenade, ready to explode, leaving unsuspecting playboys legless and broken.

Trevor Philips, on Diana, Princess of Wales, shortly before her
death in 1997

He's a world expert on leisure. He's been practising for most of his adult life.

Neil Kinnock, British politician, on Prince Philip

No danger. For no man would take away my life to make you king.

Charles II, to his brother James, Duke of York,
on the king risking assassination

I cannot but conclude the bulk of your natives to be the most pernicious race of
little odious vermin that nature ever suffered to crawl upon the surface of the
earth.

> *Jonathan Swift,* Gulliver's Travels—*the King of Brobdingnag rails*
> *against the English*

Henry VIII perhaps approached as nearly to the ideal standard of perfect
wickedness as the infirmities of human nature will allow.

> *Sir James Mackintosh, on the English king*

...a pig, an ass, a dunghill, the spawn of an adder, a basilisk, a lying buffoon, a
mad fool with a frothy mouth... a bubberly ass...

> *Martin Luther, architect of the German Reformation,*
> *on the English king Henry VIII*

The plain truth is, that he was a most intolerable ruffian, a disgrace to human
nature, and a blot of blood and grease upon the history of England.

> *Charles Dickens, about Henry VIII*

A cherub's face, a reptile all the rest.

> *Alexander Pope, about Lord Hervey*

His intellect is no more use than a pistol packed in the bottom of a trunk if one
were attacked in the robber-infested Apennines.

> *Prince Albert, on his son, the feckless Bertie—later Edward VII*

No more bloody wars, no more bloody medals.

> *Queen Mary, during World War I, on overhearing a soldier onto whose tunic she had just pinned a medal say to his neighbor, "No more bloody wars, mate."*

Dr. Donne's verses are like the peace of God: they pass all understanding.

> *King James I, on the poet John Donne*

I married the Duke for better or worse, but not for lunch.

> *The Duchess of Windsor, to a nosy person enquiring why she and the Duke dined apart at lunchtime*

He should worry—I had to ask Baldwin.

> *The Duchess of Windsor, in response to a newspaper headline of the day, which read "Harewood asks Queen for permission to marry"*

It made me feel that Albert had married beneath his station.

> *Noël Coward, on a poor stage portrayal of Queen Victoria*

My Lord, we had forgot the fart.

> *Elizabeth I of England, to Edward de Vere, Earl of Oxford, as he bowed low to greet the queen—in front of whom, years earlier, he had had the misfortune to break wind. His shame had driven him abroad, but the queen evidently recalled the occasion with amusement. Recounted in John Aubrey's* Brief Lives

A harpooned walrus.

F. E. Smith, British Conservative MP, on Lord Derby

Prince Charles's ears are so big he could hang-glide over the Falklands.

Joan Rivers

A strange, horrible business, but I suppose good enough for Shakespeare's day.

Queen Victoria passing comment on King Lear

The idea of Prince Charles conversing with vegetables is not quite so amusing
when you remember that he's had plenty of practice chatting to members of
his own family.

Jaci Stephens

She's a dumb broad.

Sue Mengers, Hollywood agent, on Princess Margaret

No, it is better not. She will only ask me to take a message to Albert.

*Benjamin Disraeli, British Conservative leader, prime minister and novelist,
declining an offer of a visit from Queen Victoria as he lay on his deathbed*

Queen Victoria was like a great paperweight that for half a century sat upon
men's minds and when she was removed their ideas began to blow all over
the place haphazardly.

H. G. Wells

Please don't touch the exhibits.

> *The Queen Mother, to a group of Australians who were*
> *clustering a little too close to her royal party while on a state visit*
> *to Australia*

Such an attractive lass. So outdoorsy. She loves nature in spite of what it did
to her.

> *Bette Midler, on Princess Anne*

Hay. And hay is for horses.

> *Tommy de Maio, New York hair stylist, on Princess Anne's hair*

I cannot find it in me to fear a man who took ten years a-learning of his
alphabet.

> *Elizabeth I of England, on Philip II of Spain*

It's like saying adultery is all right as long as you don't enjoy it.

> *Prince Philip, to an anti-hunt campaigner who had confessed to eating meat*

He speaks to me as if I were a public meeting.

> *Queen Victoria, on Gladstone*

We invite people like that to tea, but we don't marry them.

> *Lady Chetwode, on her future son-in-law, the poet John Betjeman*

As just and merciful as Nero and as good a Christian as Mahomet.

John Wesley, English clergyman, on Elizabeth I of England

If this is the way Queen Victoria treats her convicts, she doesn't deserve to
have any.

Oscar Wilde, on being incarcerated in Reading Gaol

The most insensitive and brazen pay claim in the last two hundred years.

Willie Hamilton, member of parliament, on the request of Queen Elizabeth II
that the number of people on the Civil List (i.e., paid out of the public wallet,
via the monarch's purse) be reviewed by Parliament in 1972

The wisest fool in Christendom.

Henri IV, French king, on James I of England

Dickie, you're so crooked that if you swallowed a nail you'd s**t a corkscrew.

Sir Gerald Templer to Lord Louis Mountbatten

Here lies our mutton-loving [womanizing] King,
 Whose word no man relies on.
 Who never said a foolish thing,
 And never did a wise one.

The Earl of Rochester, suggesting an epitaph for the English king Charles II.
To which the monarch is said to have replied, "True, for my words are my
own, but my deeds are my ministers'."

History

Demosthenes: "The Athenians will kill you some day when they are in a rage."
Phocion: "And you, when they are in their senses."

The barbarians who broke up the Roman Empire did not arrive a day too soon.

Ralph Waldo Emerson, Conduct of Life

We owe to the Middle Ages the two worst inventions of humanity—gunpowder and romantic love.

André Maurois, French writer and politician

Everything's at sea—except the Fleet.

Horace Walpole

A cold-blooded, calculating, unprincipled usurper, without a virtue; no statesman, knowing nothing of commerce, political economy or civil government, and supplying ignorance by bold presumption.

Thomas Jefferson, on Napoleon Bonaparte

Why did Napoleon behave in the way he did? First of all, by all accounts, he was a bit of a short-arse and you know what they say about small men. They only come up to your Adam's apples and don't like it so they have to compensate by becoming Emperor of France.

Jo Brand

I think it would be a very good idea.

Mahatma Gandhi's response to a journalist who had asked the Indian leader what he thought of Western civilization

That garrulous monk.

Benito Mussolini, on Adolf Hitler

I thought him fearfully ill-educated and quite tenth rate—pathetic. I felt quite maternal to him.

Hugh Walpole, on meeting Adolph Hitler in 1925

Quite so. But I have not been on a ship for 15 years and they still call me "Admiral."

Italian host to Eva Peron, who had complained that someone in the crowd had shouted out "Whore!" to her

Mme. de Genlis, in order to avoid the scandal of coquetry, always yielded easily.

Charles-Maurice de Talleyrand, French statesman, on a woman of letters in his day

He is a silk stocking filled with dung.

The French emperor Napoleon Bonaparte on
Charles-Maurice de Talleyrand, his foreign minister

With all my heart. Whose wife shall it be?

John Horne Tooke, to the suggestion that he should take a wife

What shall we do with this bauble? There, take it away.

Oliver Cromwell, Lord Protector of England, dissolving
Parliament in 1653

I like Lady H. too well not to wish that she had never learned to sing, for
certainly her talents do not lie that way.

Lady Palmerston, of Lady Emma Hamilton, mistress of Horatio
Nelson, in 1793

That... sordid, ambitious, vain, proud, arrogant, and vindictive knave.

General Charles Lee, on George Washington

His attachment to those of his friends whom he could make useful to himself
was thoroughgoing and exemplary.

John Quincy Adams, on Thomas Jefferson

Anything more dull and commonplace it wouldn't be easy to reproduce.

The London Times *newspaper, on Abraham Lincoln's*
Gettysburg Address

My dear McClellan,

    If you don't want to use the army I should like to borrow it for a while. Yours
respectfully,

A. Lincoln

> *Abraham Lincoln, to General McClellan, in a dig at his lack of*
> *activity during the American Civil War*

An offensive exhibition of boorishness and vulgarity.

> *General McClellan, on Abraham Lincoln*

His argument is as thin as the homeopathic soup that was made by boiling the
shadow of a pigeon that had been starved to death.

> *Abraham Lincoln, on Stephen A. Douglas, his presidential opponent*

Douglas never can be president, Sir. No, Sir; Douglas never can be president, Sir.
His legs are too short, Sir. His coat, like a cow's tail, hangs too near the
ground, Sir.

> *Thomas Hart Benton, on Stephen A. Douglas, Abraham Lincoln's*
> *presidential opponent*

I wonder if I might have a translation?

> *Harold Macmillan, during a Cold War encounter with Nikita*
> *Krushschev, who had taken off his shoe and banged it on the*
> *table in violent disagreement with his speech, which had been*
> *relayed by a United Nations interpreter*

I did keep a grocery, and I did sell cotton, candles, and cigars, and sometimes whiskey; but I remember in those days Mr. Douglas was one of my best customers. Many a time have I stood on one side of the counter and sold whiskey to Mr. Douglas on the other side, but the difference between us now is this: I have left my side of the counter, but Mr. Douglas still sticks to his as tenaciously as ever.

Abraham Lincoln, on Stephen A. Douglas, his presidential opponent

The world would not be in such a snarl,
Had Marx been Groucho instead of Karl.

Irving Berlin

He was always backing into the limelight.

Lord Berners, on T. E. Lawrence, "Of Arabia." The turn of phrase was later adopted by Churchill

The facile, leather-tongued oracle of the ordinary bourgeois intelligence.

Karl Marx, on Jeremy Bentham, British political philosopher

If he was not a great man, he was at least a great poster.

Margot Asquith on Field Marshall Lord Kitchener—famous as the face on the World War I army recruitment posters bearing the slogan, "Your Country Needs You."

Only a frantic pair of moustaches.

> *T. E. Lawrence on Ferdinand Foch, French marshal in World*
> *War I*

That loud frogmouth.

> *W. C. Fields, on Italian dictator Benito Mussolini*

The greatest cross I have to bear is the cross of Lorraine.

> *Winston Churchill, referring to French wartime leader Charles de Gaulle*

An improbable creature, like a human giraffe, sniffing down his nostrils at
mortals beneath his gaze.

> *Sir Charles Wilson, Lord Moran, on Charles de Gaulle*

He looks like a female llama who has just been surprised in her bath.

> *Winston Churchill, on General de Gaulle*

In defeat, unbeatable; in victory, unbearable.

> *Winston Churchill, on Field Marshal Sir Bernard Montgomery*
> *(First Viscount Montgomery of Alamein)*

He came out for the right side of every question—always a little too late.

> *Sinclair Lewis, on US clergyman and abolitionist Henry*
> *Ward Beecher*

Dull, Duller, Dulles.

Winston Churchill, on John Foster Dulles, US Secretary of State

If I were the Prince of Peace I should choose a less provocative ambassador.

A.E. Housman, on Bertrand Russell

Madam, I have seen their backs before.

The Duke of Wellington, to a bystander when French marshals, smarting from their resounding defeat at Waterloo, turned their backs on him at Vienna

He was oppressed by metaphor, dislocated by parentheses, and debilitated by amplification.

Samuel Parr, on a speech delivered by Edmund Burke, British author and statesman

D. is a very weak-minded fellow I am afraid, and, like the feather pillow, bears the marks of the last person who has sat on him! I hear he is called in London "genial Judas!"

General Douglas Haig, on Lord Derby, secretary for war, in 1918

He was brilliant to the top of his army boots.

David Lloyd George, on Field Marshal Earl Haig

Waterloo was a battle of the first rank won by a captain of the second.

> *Victor Hugo, French writer, on the Duke of Wellington's victory at*
> *the historic Battle of Waterloo*

The only thing that they can be relied on to do is to gallop too far and too fast.

> *The Duke of Wellington, on his own cavalry troops*

The scum of the earth—they have enlisted for drink, that is the simple truth.

> *The Duke of Wellington, on his own, victorious troops*

The most infamous army I ever commanded.

> *The Duke of Wellington, on his own, victorious troops*

There is only one caricature of me that has ever caused me annoyance: Douro.

> *The Duke of Wellington, referring to his eldest son, Lord Douro*

Or a minute.

> *James McNeill Whistler, adding his dime's worth to a dining companion*
> *singing the praises of Sir Redvers Buller who, in the Boer War, had retreated*
> *across the Modder river without losing a man, a flag, or a gun*

We did not conceive it possible that even Mr. Lincoln would produce a paper so slipshod, so loose-joined, so puerile, not alone in literary construction, but in its ideas, its sentiments, its grasp. He has outdone himself.

> Chicago Times, *on Abraham Lincoln's Gettysburg Address*

Clergyman: "How did you like my sermon, Mr. Canning?"

George Canning, British prime minister: "You were brief."

Clergyman: "Yes, you know, I avoid being tedious."

George Canning: "But, you were tedious."

You and I were long friends; you are now my enemy, and I am

Yours,

B. Franklin

Benjamin Franklin, in a letter to William Strahan

His mind was a kind of extinct sulfur pit.

Thomas Carlyle, Scottish historian and essayist,
on French emperor Napoleon III

I will prove you the notoriousest traitor that ever came to the bar... thou art a
monster; thou hast an English face, but a Spanish heart... Thou art the most
vile and execrable Traitor that ever lived... I want words sufficient to express
thy viperous Treasons... Thou art an odious fellow, thy name is hateful to all
the realm of England... There never lived a viler viper upon the face of the
earth than thou.

Sir Edward Coke, to Sir Walter Raleigh, at the latter's trial
for treason

You won the election, but I won the count.

Anastasio Somoza, onetime Nicaraguan dictator

Science

We do not have to visit a madhouse to find disordered minds; our planet is the mental institution of the universe.

Johann von Goethe

Covered over with the scab of symbols... as if a hen had been scraping there.

Thomas Hobbes, referring to the algebra of British mathematician John Wallis

The fool will overturn the whole art of astronomy.

Martin Luther, on Nicolaus Copernicus's sun-centered theory of the universe

Verily, it is easier for a camel to pass through the eye of a needle than for a scientific man to pass through a door.

Sir Arthur Eddington

[One] young lady positively refused a perfectly eligible suitor simply because he
had been unable, within a given time, to produce any new idea about
squaring the circle.

> The Journal des Savants, *March 4, 1686, poking fun at attempts by
> scientists of the day to solve the problem of how to square the circle*

Hence it has seemed necessary that some mathematician should show him, by
the reverse process of reasoning, how little he understands the mathematics
from which he takes his courage; nor should we be deterred from doing this
by his arrogance which we know will vomit poisonous filth against us.

> *John Wallis, in a letter to the Dutch physician and astronomer
> Christian Huygens (in January 1659), concerning the scientific
> research of Thomas Hobbes in* De Corpore (Concerning Body)

Which two last [books] I have here in two or three leaves wholly and clearly
confuted. And I verily believe that since the beginning of the world, there has
not been, nor ever shall be, so much absurdity written in geometry.

> *Thomas Hobbes, concerning scientific treatises by John Wallis*

Your scurvy book.

> *Thomas Hobbes, on the scientific treatises in* Arithmetica Infinitorum
> *(1656) written by John Wallis*

Biologically speaking, if something bites you, it is more likely to be female.

> *Desmond Morris*

But why the crookedness of an arch should be called an angle of contact, I know
no other reason, but because Mr. Hobbes loves to call that chalk which others
call cheese.

John Wallis, on Thomas Hobbes's method of geometry

Newton's ape... Newton's toady... a hired pen.

Johann Bernoulli, on a colleague of Newton by the name of John Keill

If the whole of the English language could be considered into one word, it
would not suffice to express the utter contempt those invite who are so
deluded as to be disciples of such an imposture as Darwinism.

Francis O. Morris, English author

The head of the filthy abortion...[we should] put an end to its crawlings.

Adam Sedgwick, Darwin's geology teacher at Cambridge,
reacting to the newfangled theory of evolution

I have no patience whatever with these gorilla damnifications of humanity.

Thomas Carlyle, Scottish essayist,
on Charles Darwin's evolutionary theories

The scientific theory I like best is that the rings of Saturn are composed entirely
of lost airline luggage.

Mark Russell

As to the descent from a monkey, I should feel it no shame to have risen from such an origin. But I should feel it a shame to have sprung from one who prostituted the gifts of culture and of eloquence to the service of prejudice and of falsehood.

Thomas Henry Huxley, respected scientist of the time, defending the evolutionary theories of Darwin against the assaults by Samuel Wilberforce, Bishop of Oxford, in 1860 (a time when it was no light affair to insult a bishop). So great was the perceived outrage that one woman present, a Lady Brewster, fainted in shock

I'd have given ten conversations with Einstein for a first meeting with a pretty chorus girl.

Albert Camus

Some folks seem to have descended from the chimpanzee later than others.

Kin Hubbard

It is absurd to think that germs causing fermentation and putrefaction come from the air; the atmosphere would have to be as thick as pea soup for that.

Dr. Nicolas Joly, on Louis Pasteur's theory of germs

Sir, I have tested your machine. It adds a new terror to life and makes death a long-felt want.

Sir Herbert Beerbohm Tree, on the gramophone—an early model— he had been asked to test by its manufacturer

Don't get smart alecksy
   With the galaxy
   Leave the atom alone.

E. Y. Harburg

I presume that all true scientists have more regard for a little man with a big
   head than for a big man with a little head.

Otto Meyer, in the New York Herald, *on the dinosaur feuds going
on between palaeontologists of the 1880s*

Sigmund Freud was a half-baked Viennese quack. Our literature, culture, and
   the films of Woody Allen would be better today if Freud had never written
   a word.

Ian Shoales

I don't want an elderly gentleman from Vienna with an umbrella inflicting his
   dreams upon me.

Vladimir Nabokov, on Sigmund Freud

One of the most fabulously stupid men of our age.

Brian Appleyard, on the philosopher Bertrand Russell

Progress has its drawbacks; you can't warm your feet on a microwave.

Doug Larson

" Places "

A bitter, strange, and inscrutable place.

Martin Amis, British novelist, on London, England

Here I am once more in this scene of dissipation and vice, and I begin already to find my morals corrupted.

Jane Austen, speaking of London in a letter to her sister
Cassandra, in August 1796

London, that great cesspool into which all the loungers of the Empire are irresistibly drained.

Sir Arthur Conan Doyle, A Study in Scarlet

When it's three o'clock in New York, it's still 1938 in London.

Bette Midler

New York: a third-rate Babylon.

H. L. Mencken

If there ever was an aviary overstocked with jays it is that Yaptown-on-the-
Hudson called New York.

O. Henry

Bugger Bognor.

George V, famously casting a shadow on that English seaside
town on his deathbed

It requires a surgical operation to get a joke well into a Scotch understanding.
The only idea of wit, or rather that inferior variety of the electric talent which
prevails occasionally in the North, and which, under the name of "Wut," is so
infinitely distressing to people of good taste, is laughing immoderately at
stated intervals.

Reverend Sydney Smith, British clergyman, 18th century

I look upon Switzerland as an inferior sort of Scotland.

Rev. Sydney Smith, British clergyman, 18th century

In Italy for 30 years under the Borgias they had warfare, terror, murder,
bloodshed—they produced Michelangelo, Leonardo da Vinci, and the
Renaissance. In Switzerland they had brotherly love, five hundred years of
democracy and peace, and what did they produce...? The cuckoo clock.

Orson Welles, in the movie The Third Man

Switzerland is simply a large, humpy, solid rock, with a thin skin of grass
stretched over it.

Mark Twain

To me, though, the symbol of Switzerland is that large middle-class female
behind. It is the most respectable thing in the world. It is deathless. Everyone
has one in this hotel; some of the elderly ladies have two.

*Katherine Mansfield, in a letter to Lady Ottoline Morrell, English
society hostess and member of the Bloomsbury group*

Scotland: That garret of the earth—That knuckle-end of England—That land of
Calvin, oat-cakes, and sulfur.

Rev. Sydney Smith, British clergyman, 18th century

Norway, too, has noble wild prospects; and Lapland is remarkable for prodigious
noble wild prospects. But, sir, let me tell you, the noblest prospect which a
Scotchman ever sees, is the high road that leads him to England.

Dr. Samuel Johnson, A Journey to the Western Islands of
Scotland

Dr. Johnson: "Sir, it is a very vile country."
Mr. S: "Well, Sir, God made it."
Dr. Johnson: "Certainly He did, but we must remember that He made it for
Scotchmen."

Dr. Samuel Johnson, A Journey to the Western Islands of
Scotland

Much may be made of a Scotchman, if he be caught young.

Dr. Samuel Johnson

I have been trying all my life to like Scotchmen, and am obligated to desist from
the experiment in despair.

Charles Lamb, English essayist

Hull is other people.

Jonathan Cecil, British actor, paraphrasing Jean-Paul Sartre's
"Hell is other people." Hull, home to the poet Philip Larkin,
had done little to merit the insult

One has not great hopes for Birmingham. I always say there is something direful
in the sound.

The character Mrs. Elton, in the novel Emma *by Jane Austen,*
on that city in the English Midlands

The surest way out of Manchester is notoriously a bottle of Gordon's Gin.

Hector Bolitho, on that city in the north of England

A relatively small and eternally quarrelsome country in Western Europe,
fountainhead of rationalist political manias, militarily impotent, historically
inglorious during the past century, democratically bankrupt, Communist-
infiltrated from top to bottom.

William F. Buckley, Jr., on France

I do not dislike the French from the vulgar antipathy between neighboring
nations, but for their insolent and unfounded airs of superiority.

Horace Walpole

Going to war without the French is like going deer-hunting without your
accordion.

Norman Schwarzkopf

The French are sawed-off sissies who eat snails, and slugs, and cheese that
smells like people's feet. Utter cowards who force their own children to drink
wine, they gibber like baboons when you try to speak to them in their own
wimpy language.

P. J. O'Rourke

France is a dog-hole.

William Shakespeare, All's Well That Ends Well

I have just defined the 100% American as 99% an idiot. And they just adore me.

George Bernard Shaw

England is a nation of shopkeepers.

Napoleon Bonaparte

The English have no exalted sentiments. They can all be bought.

Napoleon Bonaparte

It is cowardly to commit suicide. The English often kill themselves—it is a
malady caused by the humid climate.

Napoleon Bonaparte

German is the most extravagantly ugly language—it sounds likes someone using
a sick bag on a 747.

Willy Rushton, writer

Americans always try to do the right thing—after they've tried everything else.

Winston Churchill

The way to endure summer in England is to have it framed and glazed in a
comfortable room.

Horace Walpole

France is a country where the money falls apart in your hands and you can't tear
the toilet paper.

Billy Wilder

Toilet paper too thin, newspapers too fat.

Winston Churchill, on America

I found there a country with 32 religions and only one sauce.

Talleyrand, French statesman under Napoleon, on America

Frenchmen resemble apes who, climbing up a tree from branch to branch, never pause until they arrive at the highest branch, and there show their bare behinds.

Michel de Montaigne, French essayist

Nobody can simply unite a country that has 365 different kinds of cheese.

Charles de Gaulle, on his native France

Never criticize Americans. They have the best taste that money can buy.

Miles Kington, British author

There is such a thing as too much couth.

S. J. Perelman, on England

I would have loved it—without the French.

D. H. Lawrence, English writer, on France

The French probably invented the very notion of discretion. It's not that they feel that what you don't know won't hurt you; they feel that what you don't know won't hurt them. To the French lying is simply talking.

Fran Lebowitz

Britain is the only country in the world where the food is more dangerous than the sex.

Jackie Mason

Frustrate a Frenchman, he will drink himself to death; an Irishman, he will die
of angry hypertension; a Dane, he will shoot himself; an American, he will get
drunk, shoot you, then establish a million-dollar aid program for your relatives.
Then he will die of an ulcer.

Stanley Rudin

Walking is uniquely un-American.

Bill Bryson

They aren't much at fighting wars anymore. Despite their reputation for fashion,
their women have spindly legs. Their music is sappy. But they do know how
to whip up a plate of grub.

Mike Royko, on the French

It was wonderful to find America, but it would have been more wonderful to
miss it.

Mark Twain

Germany, the diseased world's bathhouse.

Mark Twain

The Rhine is of course tedious, the vineyards are formal and dull, and as far as I
can judge, the inhabitants of Germany are American.

Oscar Wilde, in a letter to Robert Ross

The German mind has a talent for making no mistakes but the very greatest.

Clifton Fadiman

I heard an Englishman, who had been long resident in America, declare that in following, in meeting, or in overtaking, in the street, on the road, or in the field, at the theater, the coffee-house, or at home, he had never overheard Americans conversing without the word DOLLAR being pronounced between them. Such unity of purpose...can...be found nowhere else, except...in an ants' nest.

Frances Trollope, English writer (and mother of Anthony Trollope),
A Commentary on Travels on a Mississippi Steamer

America is the only nation in history which, miraculously, has gone from barbarism to degeneration without the usual interval of civilization.

George Clemenceau, French statesman

America is a melting pot, the people at the bottom get burned while all the scum floats to the top.

Charlie King

When an heiress wants to buy a man, she at once crosses the Atlantic. The only really materialistic people I have ever met are the Europeans.

Mary McCarthy

The difference between Los Angeles and yogurt is that yogurt has a culture.

Tom Taussik, writer

I have just returned from Boston. It is the only thing to do if you find yourself up there.

Fred Allen

The trouble with America is that there are far too many wide, open spaces surrounded by teeth.

Charles Luckman

America is a large, friendly dog in a very small room. Every time it wags its tail it knocks over a chair.

Arnold Toynbee

Knavery seems to be so much the striking feature of its inhabitants that it may not in the end be an evil that they will become aliens to this country.

George III, passing judgement on the inhabitants of the colony he was about to lose—America

America... where laws and customs alike are based on the dreams of spinsters.

Bertrand Russell

The English think incompetence is the same thing as sincerity.

Quentin Crisp

The English think soap is civilization.

Heinrich von Treitschke

The English never smash in a face. They merely refrain from asking it to dinner.

Margaret Hasley, American writer

I know why the sun never sets on the British Empire: God wouldn't trust an Englishman in the dark.

Duncan Spaeth

Our trouble is that we drink too much tea. I see in this the slow revenge of the Orient, which has diverted the Yellow River down our throats.

J. B. Priestley, English writer, on the English obsession with tea

There are still parts of Wales where the only concession to gaiety is a striped shroud.

Gwyn Thomas

The English have an extraordinary ability for flying into a great calm.

Alexander Woollcott, American critic

The devil take these people and their language! They take a dozen monosyllabic words in their jaws, chew them, crunch them, and spit them out again, and call that speaking. Fortunately, they are by nature fairly silent, and although the gaze at us open-mouthed, they spare us long conversations.

Heinrich Heine, on the English

From every Englishman emanates a kind of gas, the deadly choke-damp of
boredom.

Heinrich Heine

Unmitigated noodles.

Kaiser Wilhelm II of Germany, on the English

The English take their pleasures gloomily, after the fashion of their country.

Maximilien de Béthune, Duc de Sully

I find it hard to say, because when I was there it seemed to be shut.

Clement Freud, English commentator and wit, on New Zealand

The national sport is breaking furniture.

P. J. O'Rourke, on Australia

I couldn't imagine a better place for making a film on the end of the world.

Actress Ava Gardner (attrib.), on the Australian city of Melbourne

Canada is useful only to provide me with furs.

Madame de Pompadour, after Quebec fell in 1759

A few acres of snow.

Voltaire, on Canada

This gloomy region, where the year is divided into one day and one night, lies
   entirely outside the stream of history.

W. W. Reade, on Canada

When I was there I found their jokes like their roads—very long and not very
   good, leading to a little tin point of a spire which has been remorselessly
   obvious for miles without seeming to get any nearer.

Samuel Butler, on Canada

So this is Winnipeg; I can tell it's not Paris.

Bob Edwards

Maine is as dead, intellectually, as Abyssinia. Nothing is ever heard from it.

H. L. Mencken

I don't even know what street Canada is on.

Al Capone

Poor Mexico, so far from God and so near to the United States.

Porfirio Diaz

There are few virtues which the Poles do not possess and there are few errors
   they have ever avoided.

Winston Churchill, in 1945

In Russia a man is called reactionary if he objects to having his property stolen
    and his wife and children murdered.

Winston Churchill

If I owned Texas and Hell, I would rent out Texas and live in Hell.

General Philip H. Sheridan

[Texas is] the place where there are the most cows and the least milk and the
    most rivers and the least water in them, and where you can look the farthest
    and see the least.

H. L. Mencken

Great God! This is an awful place.

Robert Falcon Scott, on the South Pole

It is by the goodness of God that in our country we have those three
    unspeakably precious things: freedom of speech, freedom of conscience, and
    the prudence never to practice either of them.

Mark Twain

In India, "cold weather" is merely a conventional phrase and has come into use
    through the necessity of having some way to distinguish between weather
    which will melt a brass doorknob and weather which will only make it mushy.

Mark Twain

I shall always be glad to have seen it—for the same reason Papa gave for being
   glad to have seen Lisbon—namely, "that it will be unnecessary ever to see
   it again."

Winston Churchill, on Calcutta, in a letter to his mother in 1896

Los Angeles is a city with the personality of a paper cup.

Raymond Chandler

Miami is where neon goes to die.

Lenny Bruce, comedian

The trouble with Oakland (California) is that when you get there, it's there.

Gertrude Stein

You can always reason with a German. You can always reason with a barnyard
   animal, too, for all the good it does.

P. J. O'Rourke

I am willing to love all mankind, except an American.

Rev. Sydney Smith

The national sport of England is obstacle racing. People fill their rooms with
   useless and cumbersome furniture, and spend the rest of their livings in
   trying to dodge it.

Herbert Beerbohm Tree

The English have a miraculous power to change wine into water.

Oscar Wilde, while in Paris

I once spent a year in Philadelphia, I think it was on a Sunday.

W. C. Fields

Italy, at least, has two things to balance its miserable poverty and mismanagement: a lively intellectual movement and a good climate. Ireland is Italy without these two.

James Joyce, Irish writer

It's a fact that if you stay in California you lose one point of IQ for every year.

Truman Capote

We have really everything in common with America nowadays except, of course, language.

Oscar Wilde, in The Canterville Ghost

There's nothing wrong with Southern California that a rise in ocean level wouldn't cure.

Ross MacDonald

Very little is known of the Canadian country since it's rarely visited by anyone but the Queen and illiterate sports fishermen.

P. J. O'Rourke

Mark Twain

I admire him, I frankly confess it; and when his time comes I shall buy a piece of the rope for a keepsake.

On Cecil Rhodes, dubious Empire-builder in Southern Africa

Reader, suppose you were an idiot. And suppose you were a member of congress. But I repeat myself.

On Members of Congress

He could charm an audience an hour on a stretch without ever getting rid of an idea.

On an unknown individual

Fleas can be taught nearly everything that a congressman can.

On Members of Congress

How often we recall with regret that Napoleon once shot at a magazine editor and missed him and killed a publisher. But we remember with charity that his intentions were good.

On the French Emperor Napoleon

To my mind Judas Iscariot was nothing but a low, mean, premature congressman.

In a letter to the editor of the New York Daily Tribune

Had double chins all the way down to his stomach.

On Oliver Wendell Holmes, jurist

In the first place God made idiots; this was for practice; then he made school boards.

On the school board

He is useless on top of the ground; he aught to be under it, inspiring the cabbages.

On an unknown individual

He was a solemn, unsmiling, sanctimonious old iceberg who looked like he was waiting for a vacancy in the Trinity.

On an unknown individual

Cauliflower is nothing but cabbage with a college education.

On a relatively harmless vegetable

His ignorance covers the world like a blanket, and there's scarcely a hole in it anywhere.

On an unknown individual

I could never learn to like her, except on a raft at sea with no other provisions in sight.

On an unknown individual

A banker is a fellow who lends you his umbrella when the sun is shining and wants it back the minute it begins to rain.

On movers and shakers in the world of finance

I didn't attend the funeral, but I sent a nice letter saying I approved of it.

On an unknown individual

You take the lies out of him, and he'll shrink to the size of your hat; you take the malice out of him, and he'll disappear.

On an unknown individual

Last week I stated that this woman was the ugliest woman I had ever seen. I have since been visited by her sister and now wish to withdraw that statement.

On an unknown individual

It is full of interest. It has noble poetry in it; and some clever fables; and some blood-drenched history; and some good morals; and a wealth of obscenity; and upward of a thousand lies.

On the Bible

It ain't those parts of the Bible that I can't understand that bother me, it's the parts I do understand.

On the Bible

If he were to write about an Orphan Princess who lost a Peanut, he would feel obliged to try to make somebody snuffle over it.

Attacking what he saw as the sentimentality of the writer Bret Harte

...the worst literary shoemaker I know. He is as blind as a bat. He never sees anything correctly, except Californian scenery. He is as slovenly as Thackeray, and as dull as Charles Lamb.

On the prose style of Bret Harte

Say I knew the son of a bitch.

When asked by a reporter to comment on his onetime friendship with Bret Harte

The critic's symbol should be the tumble-bug; he deposits his egg in somebody else's dung, otherwise he could not hatch it.

On literary critics

"Sport"

[It is] war without the shooting.

George Orwell, British writer, on the matter of "serious" sport

I'm not having points taken off me by an incompetent old fool. You're the pits of the world.

John McEnroe, to tennis judge Edward James

You can't see as well as these f*****g flowers—and they're f*****g plastic.

John McEnroe, to a line judge

What other problems do you have besides being unemployed, a moron, and a dork?

John McEnroe, to a spectator at a tennis match

McEnroe was as charming as always, which means that he was as charming as a dead mouse in a loaf of bread.

Clive James, Australian-born critic, about John McEnroe

He's never going to be a great player on grass. The only time he comes to the net is to shake your hand.

Goran Ivanisevic, on Ivan Lendl

He's phony, using his blackness to get his way.

Joe Frazier, about Muhammad Ali

Joe Frazier is so ugly he should donate his face to the US Bureau of Wildlife.

Muhammad Ali, about Joe Frazier

We've been trying to get Elvis. He's been dead long enough.

Ray Foreman, on finding a new opponent for boxer George Foreman

Honey, if it's all-in, why wrestle?

Mae West, to a pugilist explaining—at tedious length—his craft

Beyond the hair, tattoos, and earrings, he's just like you and me.

Bob Hill, on Dennis Rodman

Dennis has become like a prostitute, but now it's gotten ridiculous, to the point where he will do anything humanly possible to make money.

Charles Barkley, on Dennis Rodman

He has so many fishhooks in his nose, he looks like a piece of bait.

Bob Costas, on Dennis Rodman

Martina was so far in the closet she was in danger of being a garment bag.

Rita Mae Brown, on her partner Martina Navratilova

Have you heard of that part of the body called a spine? Get one!

Andy Roddick, tennis player, to an umpire

A legend in his own lunchtime.

Christopher Wordsworth, on the sporting journalist Clifford Makins

He likes to complain about not playing, which is what he does best—not play.

Pat Gillick, on pitcher Mike Marshall

He doesn't know the meaning of the word fear. In fact, I just saw his grades and he doesn't know the meaning of a lot of words.

Bobby Bowden, Florida State footballer, on player Reggie Herring

Reporter from *USA Today*: "What would you do if you retired?"
Charles Barkley, basketball star: "If push came to shove, I could lose all self-respect and become a reporter."

The designated gerbil.

Bill Lee, Boston Red Sox pitcher, on manager Don Zimmer, who favored designated batters

He could start a row in an empty house.

Sir Alex Ferguson, British football manager, on footballer Dennis Wise

The only time he opens his mouth is to change feet.

David Feherty, on Nick Faldo

He has a face like a warthog that's been stung by a wasp.

David Feherty, on fellow golfer, Colin Montgomerie

To call Keegan a superstar is stretching a point. He's been very, very lucky, an
average player who came into the game when it was short of personalities.
He's not fit to lace my boots as a player.

George Best, on footballer Kevin Keegan

Karate is a form of martial arts in which people who have had years and years of
training, can, using only their hands and feet, make some of the worst movies
in the history of the world.

Dave Barry

He couldn't bowl a hoop downhill.

Fred Trueman, on fellow cricketer, Ian Botham

A lot of people are using two-piece cues nowadays. Alex Higgins hasn't got one
because they don't come with instructions.

Steve Davis, on snooker world champion, Alex Higgins

Like a Volvo, Bjorn Borg is rugged, has good after-sales service, and is very dull.

Clive James, on tennis player Bjorn Borg

Trevor Brooking floats like a butterfly and stings like one too.

Brian Clough

Football combines the two worst features of American life: violence and
committee meetings.

George Will

I don't want to play golf. When I hit a ball, I want someone else to go chase it.

Rogers Hornsby

Golf is a game in which one endeavors to control a ball with implements ill-
adapted for the purpose.

Woodrow Wilson

I hate all sports as rabidly as a person who likes sports hates common sense.

H. L. Mencken

I never play cricket. It requires one to assume such indecent postures.

Oscar Wilde

I often take exercise. Why, only yesterday I had breakfast in bed.

Oscar Wilde

Football is all very well, a good game for rough girls, but not for delicate boys.

Oscar Wilde

If he had gunpowder for brains he couldn't blow his cap off.

Bill Shankly

Brian Clough's worse than the rain in Manchester. At least God stops that
occasionally.

Bill Shankly

You son, could start a riot in a graveyard.

Bill Shankly, to Tommy Smith

Ally MacLeod thinks that tactics are a new kind of mint.

Billy Connolly, on infamous Scotland soccer manager, Ally McLeod

I am definitely not scared of Mike Tyson. I am at the top of the food chain and
he is looking to knock me off. Mike's an arrogant imbecile. He sounds like a
cartoon character.

Lennox Lewis, heavyweight boxing champion

He must be the only man alive who can eat an apple through a tennis racket.

Gary Lineker, during the 2002 World Cup, on Ronaldo

Baseball has the great advantage over cricket of being ended sooner.

George Bernard Shaw

The American team is made up of eleven gentlemen and Paul Azinger.

Seve Ballesteros, referring to the Ryder Cup team in 1991

I think he's the jerk of the world.

> *Fred Funk, American professional golfer, in response to Colin Montgomerie,*
> *who had criticized the 1997 US Ryder Cup squad*

So what if he has the most perfect bowel movement on tour?

> *Dave Hill, on fellow golfer Gary Player's constant bragging about*
> *his physical form*

Golf is a good walk spoiled.

> *Mark Twain*

If I had my way, any man guilty of golf would be ineligible for any office of trust
in the United States.

> *H. L. Mencken*

Golf: a game in which you claim the privileges of age, and retain the playthings
of childhood.

> *Dr. Samuel Johnson*

I regard golf as an expensive way of playing marbles.

> *G. K. Chesterton*

[Playing golf is] like chasing a quinine pill around a cow pasture.

> *Winston Churchill*

Golf appeals to the idiot in us and the child. Just how childlike golf players become is proven by their frequent inability to count past five.

John Updike

The game of golf would lose a great deal if croquet mallets and billiard cues were allowed on the putting green.

Ernest Hemingway

Fifty-seven old farts...

Will Carling, on the committee making up Rugby Union's governing body

Sailing—the fine art of getting wet and becoming ill while slowly going nowhere at great expense.

Henry Beard and Roy Mckie, A Sailor's Dictionary

Like Olympic medals and tennis trophies, all they signified was that the owner had done something of no benefit to anyone more capably than everyone else.

Robert Graves

Someone with about as much charisma as a damp sparkplug.

Alan Hubbard, of the Observer, *on Nigel Mansell*

As genuine as a three-dollar bill.

Mickey Duff, on boxer Chris Eubank

Self Put Downs

There is no warm, loveable person inside; beneath my cold exterior, once you break the ice, you find cold water.

Gore Vidal, on himself

Every time I get into the newspapers, I injure myself professionally.

Norman Mailer

Take a close-up of a woman past sixty! You might as well use a picture of a relief map of Ireland.

Nancy Astor, when asked for a close-up photograph (attrib.)

I used to be Snow White... but I drifted.

Mae West

When I don't look like the tragic muse, I look like the smoky relic of the great Boston Fire.

Louisa May Alcott

The three ages of man: youth, middle age, and "You're looking well, Enoch!"

Enoch Powell

Do you think my mind is maturing late, or simply rotted early?

Ogden Nash

I'm a colored, one-eyed Jew.

*Sammy Davis, Jr., when asked during a game of golf what
his handicap was*

I know I am getting better at golf because I am hitting fewer spectators.

Gerald Ford

I'm as pure as the driven slush.

Tallulah Bankhead

George Bernard Shaw (to a member of the audience booing the first night of
his play): "My friend, I quite agree with you. But what are we two against
so many?"

My movies were the kind they show in prisons and on airplanes, because no
one can leave.

Burt Reynolds

I don't have to look up my family tree, because I know that I'm the sap.

Fred Allen—on himself

First I lost my voice, then I lost my figure, and then I lost Onassis.

Maria Callas

It took me fifteen years to discover I had no talent for writing, but I couldn't give it up because by that time I was too famous.

Robert Benchley

Drawing on my fine command of the English language, I said nothing.

Robert Benchley

The most expensive haircut I ever had cost £10... and £9 went on the search fee.

William Hague, the follicly challenged leader of the Conservative Party in Britain

It is perfectly monstrous the way people go about nowadays saying things against one, behind one's back, that are absolutely and entirely true.

Oscar Wilde

I live in terror of not being misunderstood.

Oscar Wilde

I always look skint. When I buy a *Big Issue*, people take it out of my hand and give me a pound.

Billy Connolly, British comedian

I think I mentioned to Bob [Geldof] I could make love for eight hours. What I didn't say was that this included four hours of begging and then dinner and a movie.

Sting

Jack Paar, in a TV interview with Oscar Levant in the early 1960s: "What do you do for exercise?"

Levant's reply: "I stumble and then I fall into a coma."

When I burnt my bra it took the fire department four days to put out the blaze.

Dolly Parton

An actress's life is so transitory; suddenly you're a building.

Helen Hayes, on having a theater named after her

Cocaine habit-forming? Of course not. I ought to know. I've been using it for years.

Tallulah Bankhead

When I appear in public people expect me to neigh, grind my teeth, paw the ground, and swish my tail—none of which is easy.

Princess Anne

Madam, all babies look like me.

Winston Churchill, on being told—for the umpteenth time—by a bystander that her baby "looks just like you"

Being an old maid is like death by drowning, a really delightful sensation after
you cease to struggle.

Edna Ferber

Gloomy old sod, aren't I?

Philip Larkin, British poet

Everything I've ever said will be credited to Dorothy Parker.

George S. Kaufman

I not only muck up some of my plays by writing them but I frequently muck
them up by acting in them as well.

Noël Coward

I don't know anything about music. In my line, you don't have to.

Elvis Presley

If people only knew as much about painting as I do, they would never buy my
pictures.

Sir Edwin Henry Landseer, English painter, to W. P. Frith

It takes a lot of money to look this cheap.

Dolly Parton

Somebody's boring me. I think it's me.

Dylan Thomas, Welsh poet

I seem to be better when I keep my mouth shut. Maybe I should move into
silent films.

Helena Bonham-Carter, actress

When I am in the pulpit, I have the pleasure of seeing my audience nod
approbation while they sleep.

Rev. Sidney Smith, onetime canon of St Paul's Cathedral, London

I think I may boast myself to be, with all possible vanity, the most unlearned
and uninformed female who ever dared to be an authoress.

Jane Austen, in a letter to the Rev. James Clarke

I am a gentleman: I live by robbing the poor.

George Bernard Shaw

I have the face and body of a woman and the mind of a child.

Elizabeth Taylor

Why, Aaron, you're becoming an egomaniac. You used to be able to listen to me
all night.

*Oscar Levant, to composer Aaron Copeland, who he had been
subjecting to a long lecture—Copeland got up to leave*

You have but two topics, yourself and me, and I'm sick of both.

Dr. Samuel Johnson, to James Boswell, his devoted chronicler

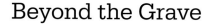

Beyond the Grave

Beneath this stone, a lump of clay
  Lies Arabella Young
  Who on the 21st of May
  Began to hold her tongue.

Epitaph in a churchyard in Hatfield, Massachusetts

Here lies my wife; here let her lie!
  Now she's at rest, and so am I.

John Dryden, Epitaph Intended for Dryden's Wife

Here lies Bernard Lightfoot, who was accidentally killed in the 45th year of
  his age.
  This monument was erected by his grateful family.

Epitaph on a soldier in a rural English churchyard

Here lies

Ezekial Aikle

Aged 102

The Good

Die Young

Epitaph in East Dalhousie, Nova Scotia

I bequeath all my property to my wife on the condition that she remarry
immediately. Then there will be at least one man to regret my death.

Heinrich Heine, German poet and essayist

Only think of Mrs. Holder's being dead! Poor woman, she has done the one
thing in the world she could possibly do to make one cease to abuse her.

Jane Austen, English author, in a letter to her
sister Cassandra

She was never really charming until she died.

Terence, classical writer, in an epitaph for an unknown woman

She sleeps alone at last.

Robert Benchley, suggesting an epitaph for a gadabout actress

Howard Hughes was the only man I ever knew who had to die to prove that he
had been alive.

Walter Kane

Acknowledgments

The author would like to thank the staff at the British Library, where much of this book was researched and written—and the friends, family, and publishing colleagues who donated their halfpenny's worth with recollections of acerbic anecdotes and squelching put downs plus fruitful leads on where to dig.

Some of the quotes between these covers have appeared in a number of anthologies, while others seem so perfectly fashioned for the English language that they have been taken into everyday speech, with the original pronouncer and/or wording all-but lost in the mists of time. The realm of "acid wit" is vast, rich, and apparently inexhaustible, and has it seems, gained innumerable eager eavesdroppers and recorders. The author is indebted to those researchers, compilers, archivists, authors, and editors who have thus enriched the pool that is the commonwealth of curmudgeonly quotes.